Dear Reader,

The World Cup is coming! A fiesta of football! A veritable couch potato carnival!

And it's in Brazil, the home of *jogo bonito*, the beautiful game. Brazil, the land of silky samba-style soccer and sun-kissed senhoritas!

And what's more, England have qualified to take their well-deserved place at the top table of world football, having put the might of Montenegro, Moldova and San Marino in their places – wherever they may be.

And yet for some reason the nation seems shrouded in apathy, apprehension, resignation, doom and gloom.

But why is this? How can this be?

Are we so jaded with the massive over-abundance of live football on telly that even a World Cup feels like just another square-eyed endurance test?

Are we so disillusioned with the way football has repeatedly sold its soul for money that footballers no longer seem like heroes to us, but rather bloated and distant sleeve-tattooed buffoons, paid obscene amounts of dosh simply for being able to balance a pig bladder on their neck or make a referee believe they have been tripped up when they haven't?

Are we so depressed by the utter remoteness of any chance of England even hinting at coming close to winning the thing, now that the 'golden' generation have finally hung up their wallets, that we can hardly bear to bring ourselves to watch?

Well, of course. All of these things.

But this is the World Cup, and World Cups are the vivid staging posts of a life spent in love with the beautiful game. Who can forget Geoff Hurst slamming the ball against the bar and turning away in triumph? Carlos Alberto smashing his daisy cutter in to make it four for Brazil? The Cruyff turn? The Ardiles backheel? Marco Tardelli's insane gallop of celebration? Maradona's pat-a-ball mugging of Peter Shilton? Roger Milla dancing with the corner flag? Hard man Stuart Pearce in tears? Slightly less hard man Roberto Baggio's Diana Ross tribute penalty kick? Beckham sent off? Ronaldinho's floating leaf? Rooney sent off? And the triumph of tiki-taka in the rainbow country? What unforgettable images will be burned indelibly onto our memory retinas this time?

We owe it to ourselves, and to our children, and to our children's children, not to let the World Cup pass by unremarked. We need to make the most of it, make it a life-enhancing experience.

We need to *enjoy* it. And here's how...

Yours,

Chris England*

---

* Yes, it's my real name.

HOW to ENJOY The World Cup

CHRIS ENGLAND

WITH ILLUSTRATIONS BY JAMES NUNN

Old St

Also by Chris England

Balham to Bollywood
An Evening with Gary Lineker
Breakfast with Jonny Wilkinson
No More Buddha, Only Football
What Didn't Happen Next

First published in 2014 by Old Street Publishing Ltd,
Trebinshun House, Brecon LD3 7PX
www.oldstreetpublishing.co.uk

ISBN 978 1 908699 91 6

10 9 8 7 6 5 4 3 2 1

A CIP catalogue record for this title is available from the British Library.
Printed and bound by CPI Group (UK) Ltd, Croydon, CR0 4YY

For my sons

CONTENTS

So let's see – what do you really need to enjoy the World Cup? What do you want?

FACTS, FACTS, FACTS!

And you will get them. There's a double-page spread of information about all 32 teams, little titbits you can drop into conversation down the pub or in front of the TV, plus all the scheduling details, including what match is being played where and on what channel. Plus lots of other stuff. Because being a know-all is always enjoyable, isn't it?

HOW TO PREPARE MENTALLY

This feature will help you to prepare yourself mentally to enjoy the World Cup. With the help of Dr Zaius, you will learn to ignore certain aspects of the whole affair – the blurtings of Sepp Blatter, the blatant commercialism, the jingoism, your country's image being represented by sunburned alcoholics in three-quarter length shorts, etc, etc, etc.

HOW TO PICK A SECOND TEAM

All the pre-tournament information you could want about every participating nation, in order to enable you to pick a second team to follow. Just in case the England adventure is cut disappointingly short.

HOW TO ENJOY THE WORLD CUP IF YOU'RE A PARENT, AN ASTRONAUT, A POLITICIAN . . . OR SCOTTISH

Wholesome Outdoor Activities

PRACTISE YOUR WORLD CUP SKILLS

There will be at least **7,830 minutes** of football played during this World Cup, so it falls to me to deliver this Health and Safety warning: get up off your blinking backsides before they become grafted to your sofa!

What better way to get some fresh air and stay fit for the televisual overload ahead than to pop out to the garden or the local park between games and practise the brilliant individual skills from previous World Cup tournaments?

HOW TO EAT AND DRINK – BRAZILIAN STYLE

We can't all make it all the way down to the Copacabana, but we can kick back in the garden with an ice-cool *caipirinha* and enjoy a sizzling *churrasco*. Piranha soup, anyone?

LEARN TO READ THE NIGHT SKY

This bonus astronomy section points out some little-known footballing constellations that illuminate the night sky every four years, at World Cup time.

Wholesome Indoor Activities

HOW TO CREATE A WORLD CUP PLAYLIST

Three world cup playlists, in fact. One with Brazilian tunes, one with English ones, and a third featuring music from around the world. Plus some classic football movies to watch.

THE ULTIMATE WORLD CUP WALLCHART

How to make yourself a world-class World Cup wallchart that will amaze your friends and galvanize your children's interest, respect and admiration as you successfully manage to download some bits and pieces off our website.

WORLD CUP COLLECTABLES

All you need to know about World Cup memorabilia, including what you might be able to pick up from previous tournaments, and what our leading petrol stations might have in store for us this time round.

WORLD CUP DRINKING GAME

OK, so strictly speaking this one might not count as wholesome. Unless maybe you play it with guava juice.

Plus ...

WORLD CUP I-SPY

Things to watch out for once the tournament is underway, with a complicated points scoring system that will automatically enhance your World Cup enjoyment.

VOODOO-TEO

How to destroy England's enemies using the power of Voodoo-teo (honest).

QUIZZES

Three fiendish quizzes to test your footballing expertise. Along with the traditional answers at the back.

THREE STORIES FROM 1950, WHEN THE WORLD CUP LAST CAME TO BRAZIL

BBC vs ITV

Another enjoyable (if faintly nerdy) aspect of a World Cup is observing how the two main national broadcasters go head-to-head. But who will emerge victorious? Lineker or Chiles?

So come on, let's enjoy the World Cup together. Remember – it's supposed to be fun!

MENTAL PREPARATION

'Fail to prepare
mentally,
prepare to
be a mental
failure'

During the build-up to the World Cup, Roy Hodgson tried to divert attention from the inexplicable selection of Tom Cleverly by hiring a sports psychologist.

Dr Steve Peters is the author of a help-yourself book called *The Chimp Paradox*. The idea is that your brain is made up of the 'human' – the rational side – and the 'chimp' – the emotional side. Apparently, to improve your performance, you should try to 'cage the chimp'.

I thought this approach might work for fans as well as players, so I found a psychologist who claimed to be versed in 'Chimp Theory', and booked an appointment.

Dr Zaius turned out to be a hairy man, very hairy, with lots of hair everywhere – on his head, on his chin, on his feet, and sprouting from the cuffs of his jacket.

I explained that I wanted to learn how to 'cage the chimp', so that I could enjoy the World Cup to the maximum. Dr Zaius instantly became very agitated.

"No, no!" he screeched, baring his teeth and thumping his chest. "It is the human that must be caged! Alone among God's primates he kills for sport!"

"I think I see," I said. "You are saying that I must learn to suppress my human, logical side? And basically not think of all the things that wind me up about the World Cup, and about football generally?"

"Ahem... yes, that's it exactly, that's what I meant..."

"And you can help me with that?" I asked.

"Very well," Dr Zaius said, lighting up. "I'll see what I can do."

So here are **ten things to avoid thinking about** if you want to enjoy the 2014 World Cup, along with Dr Zaius's helpful tips.

1. Try not to think about England's chances.

Traditionally England go into a major tournament as one of the favourites, on account of the number of poor deluded souls who whack their hard-earned on the home team in defiance of common sense or the evidence of their own eyes. Such hopelessly unrealistic hopes are a sure recipe for non-enjoyment when they turn out to be... well... hopelessly unrealistic.

 Dr Zaius says: 'Think about this. If you can reduce your expectations sufficiently then any little success can give you pleasure – winning a corner, stringing three passes together... If you expect nothing, then it's harder to be disappointed. Also Roy Hodgson should definitely not pick Tom Cleverley or Chris Smalling. And Rooney can't be the lone striker, that's just blindingly obvious.'

2. Try not to think about metatarsal misery.

There's always one or two key players who pick up some sort of injury that rules them out of the tournament, or (worse) rules them *into* the tournament but only after weeks of stories about how they are sleeping in an oxygen tent to help speed up their recovery. It used to be Bryan Robson, then it was Gazza, then David Beckham, then Wayne Rooney and Michael Owen. So far we've lost Theo Walcott entirely, and Jack Wilshere is in that ghastly netherland of uncertainty...

 Dr Zaius says: 'Think about this. Football, especially international football, is a squad game, and it's rare that one player is so good that all your hopes rest on him. Indeed, sometimes necessity is the mother of invention. If Bobby Robson hadn't lost Bryan Robson (when his arm fell off) and Ray Wilkins (to suspension), would he have stumbled upon the partnership of Glenn Hoddle and Peter Reid, which worked much better? And Rio Ferdinand and Sol Campbell pulling out of Euro 2004 meant Sven found John Terry and Ledley King.'

3. Try not to think about the 'Group of Geoff'.

England are in a tough group, no doubt about it. Uruguay and Italy are both teams that could realistically go a long way in the tournament, while Costa Rica are a banana skin waiting to happen.

Dr Zaius says: 'Think about this. It's not going to be easy, but it is by no means impossible. Uruguay were unimpressive in qualifying, and have an ageing defence that may well leak goals. Italy's form is patchy. Plus, they are serial bus-parkers and a draw might be enough against them. And don't talk to me about banana skins, I know all about them. The trick is to pick them up and put them straight in the recycling.'

4. Try not to think about how much money footballers are paid.

This is tricky, given how much the newspapers bang on about it. What gets me is how they always express footballers' pay in how much it is *per week*, as though there were still some connection between today's players and the working-class heroes of yesteryear.

Are we really expected to believe that Wayne Rooney collects £300k in a brown envelope from the lady in the admin office every Friday afternoon?

 Dr Zaius says: 'Think about this. At least at the World Cup itself the players are not being paid astronomical sums. Of course some of them will make a name for themselves at the tournament and will thus be paid astronomical sums thereafter, so I suppose those players can be thought of as being motivated by money. And you do always hear stories about one or other of the teams (usually Russia) promising their players bizarre win bonuses, like a tractor. By and large, though, the players in Brazil will be playing for national pride, and glory, and the thrill of performing on the world stage. So: enjoy!'

5. Try not to think about the Premiership.

Of all the things that have made football worse than it used to be, the top one is this. In 1992 English football set about the miserable mean-spirited business of reorganising itself so that the point of every football season was to arrange all the clubs in the country in order of how rich they were. The sport's administrators cravenly caved in to vested interests, failing to protect the game's integrity, with the result that there is now a playing field so uneven that it makes the Himalayas look like a village bowling green. It's depressing.

 Dr Zaius says: 'Think about this. No nation can be taken over by Russian billionaires (not even

Russia) and bankrolled to victory. No national team can poach Robin van Persie (say) by offering to pay him more cash. Some nations are richer than others, of course they are. Some are simply bigger, with a greater pool of talent to draw upon. But in the end, the World Cup will go to the one with the best bunch of footballers this time. And it could be Belgium, which would be funny.'

6. Try not to think about the Champions League.

This bloated sponsorship-and-ad-fest squats over European football like an ugly cash-munching toad. It is not really a competition at all. It is a hugely depressing and self-perpetuating financial cycle. Clubs have to be in the thing or else they risk "not matching the ambitions" of the top players they need in order to stay in the thing. Television companies are obliged to show hours and hours of endless unimportant matches. Meanwhile my elderly mother tries to work out where *Emmerdale* has gone.

 Dr Zaius says: 'Think about this. At the World Cup teams can get eliminated very quickly, and after that it's knockout games all the way, with nail-biters and penalty shootouts, and football that actually means something. The World Cup is so much better than the Champions League it is almost like it's another sport entirely.'

7. Try not to think about Sepp Blatter.

He runs FIFA, an organisation with the budget of a medium-sized country, and which is accountable to no one, yet Sepp Blatter's only credential for being in charge of football is that his head looks a bit like one. His previous administrative experience is as the chairman of an organisation dedicated to persuading women to wear stockings instead of pantyhose.

Blatter's every move is dictated by money or by votes, or by using one to get the other, and his tenure has been subject to constant criticism and insinuations of corrupt practices that would not look out of place in Zimbabwe (say), but he's still there, still in charge. It's not that the mud doesn't stick. It's just that he utterly refuses to go along with the idea that being muddy is bad.

 Dr Zaius says: 'Think about this. I like the sound of this fellow – he's got some good ideas. He's very old, though, and can't go on forever... can he? Unfortunately the nature of FIFA – a vast cash-producing monolith answerable to no one – makes it virtually impossible that a white knight with a spotless reputation will ever be able to ride in and clean the place up. The best you can hope for is someone not quite so objectionable. Because if Blatter decides to follow the example of the Roman Emperor Tiberius and grooms a successor that will make this look like a kind of golden age, then Heaven help us all. Who could possibly be worse, though? Mugabe? Is this helpful?'

8. Try not to think about the Official Partners of 2014 FIFA World Cup Brazil ™.

This is a scheme that FIFA have come up with to get money out of big corporate sponsors, and it is pretty irritating. It means that these corporate sponsors, like Coca-Cola and McDonalds (say), get to stick the World Cup logo on everything. They also have a monopoly on what is sold in the venues and the fan parks. If you want to buy a ticket, you need to pay by Visa (the Official Credit Card of the World Cup). If you want a beer it'd better bc a Bud. And if you wear a logo that is not an Adidas one you'd better be prepared to cover up or disrobe or get thrown out.

 Dr Zaius says: 'Think about this. If you are watching at home even Sepp Blatter can't tell you what to do. So find out who the Official Partners are, and get whatever it is you want from someone else. Unless you really fancy a Blg Mac, of course, now that they're on your mind, or a Coke for that matter. And if you're out of cash then paying with a Visa might just be the handiest thing. Plus you've already got your Adidas trainers on, so...'

9. Try not to think about the stadia.

As usual, FIFA has required the host nation to produce glittering new stadia. Gone are the days when the World Cup would roll up and take advantage of characterful history-soaked venues that already existed. No, no – where would be the potential for kickbacks in that scenario? So Brazil have had to deliver a dozen brand spanking new and monstrously expensive grounds.

The strong likelihood is that these stadia will be under-used white elephants in years to come. So why build them at all? Either a nation can put on a World Cup or it can't, and wouldn't you rather see games played in the colourful and idiosyncratic stadia used every week, than in soulless identikit concrete bowls with moving advertising boards that could be anywhere in the world? You would? Well, tough.

Dr Zaius says: 'Think about this. However depressing it is to see Brazil's people held to ransom to provide these unnecessary new facilities, it may well be even worse next time and the time after. Russia is sure to be every bit as bad, while Qatar is already mired in some ghastly slave-labour scandals. And there's still eight years to go.'

10. Try not to think about the England Band.

Easier said than done, as their brain-battering racket forms the audio backdrop to every England game, courtesy of tickets provided by the F.A., who have somehow got the impression that everybody loves these barely competent parpists.

Dr Zaius says: 'Think about this. Actually you're right, that England band is really annoying, and you can't turn the sound down on the telly without robbing yourself of the atmosphere and the commentary too. You could try listening to the radio commentary – the parpists might not be so noticeable there – but it's not always in sync with the pictures, and in my experience you can still hear the bastards. 'The Great Escape', I really hate that one, and the bloody 'Self-Preservation Society', and then 'The Great Escape' again! If I had my way they'd all be taken to The Forbidden Zone and left to rot.'

* * *

I then told Dr Zaius that the England band had started practising the old samba-style classic 'Brazil', and were planning to play it non-stop for ninety minutes whenever England were playing.

He became very worked up, leaping over his desk to grab me by the shirt front. I told him to take his stinking mitts off me, then he jumped on top of his filing cabinet and began pelting me with his own excrement. Which wasn't very professional.

I think a lot of the certificates on Dr Zaius's wall were off of the internet.

HOW TO ENJOY THE WORLD CUP

IF YOU ARE... a *Parent*

When I was a kid I used to absolutely hoover up any football highlights on the goggle box – *Match of the Day, The Big Match, Sportsnight* (with or without Coleman). Live televised football was a rare treat indeed. There was the Cup final, of course, and the Home Internationals, and the occasional Wembley qualifier, but apart from that it was just the four-yearly fix of the World Cup. And even then there was no guarantee that England would have managed to qualify for it.

Kids today – well, they don't know they're born. The Premiership, The Champions League, the Europa League, the F.A. Cup right from the really early rounds – there's so much televised football that it's actually hard for kids to get into it at all.

Football these days is too demanding. You can't possibly watch it all, so why watch any of it? By chasing the big bucks football has turned itself into something the younger generation can either take or leave – and these are the potential season-ticket holders of the future we are talking about.

We can't trust the custodians of the game to take care of its future, not while there are sponsorship deals to be done and television rights to sell. It's up to us, as parents, to make sure our kids can get the pleasure that we've got from the beautiful game in years to come. It's not enough to shrug and let them mooch about on Facebook, or whatever.

There's a World Cup on for God's sake!

Sprinkled throughout this volume are things you can do to draw your children into this kick-a-ball extravaganza. And once they are hooked, they are football's for life!

Take a look at **The Ultimate World Cup Wall Chart**, **How to Create a World Cup Sticker Album**, plus all the **World Cup Skills** sections. And many more (as Ronco would say)!

And if you have a kid who is interested in cooking (you must be very proud), then why not let him or her loose on some of the **World Cup food and drink ideas** in the book?

WORLD CUP SKILLS #1

The Blanco Hop

All-time great Mexico star Cuauhtémoc Blanco, who won 119 caps, and spent most of his club career turning out for Club América, invented this tremendous surprise manoeuvre, and he stunned the watching world with it at the 1998 World Cup.

The Blanco Hop – also known as the *Cuauhteminha* – comes into its own when you are faced with two defenders, who have foolishly left a gap between them wide enough to hop through. You grasp the ball between your ankles, and then you leap forwards into the air clutching it up beneath your backside. You should have sufficient momentum to pass between your startled opponents. You will also need to take advantage of the crucial split seconds that it will take them to lift their bottom jaws from the turf to pick up enough speed to actually get away from them once you land.

When Blanco did this against Italy the shock value was greatly increased by the fact that he bounced clean over an almost-equally trademark scythe tackle by Italy's Zambrotta that could have taken his leg off.

15

BRAZIL IN FACTS #1

It's where the nuts come from

That is, according to the famous quotation from Lord Fancourt 'Babbs' Babberly, a posh twit character in Brandon Thomas's massively popular 1892 farce *Charley's Aunt*.

Brazil nuts, the Incredible Hulk of the mixed-nut multiverse, are not, botanically speaking, nuts – as Stephen Fry is doubtless telling you on *Dave* (or possibly *Dave Ja Vu*) at this very moment. They are seeds. Technically the nut is the hard casing, the size of a coconut, that grows near the top of the roughly 150-foot Brazil tree, and which contains maybe 20 or 30 of what we mistakenly think of as the Brazil nuts fitting together like the segments of an orange. These nut cases are hefty enough to kill you if one lands on your head. Your family would not be able to sue the plantation owner, however, as Brazil nuts only grow in the wild. Their pollination is dependent on a particular species of long-tongued bee, which in turn is attracted by a particular type of wild orchid.

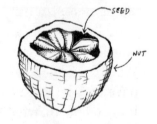

Bolivia is actually top of the league table for producing Brazil nuts, although Brazil qualified fairly comfortably in second place and are tipped to go all the way in the knockout stages.

Once upon a time Brazil nuts were known as 'n-----toes', where the n-word is a word you can't use any more. You can see them advertised as such, somewhat alarmingly if you don't know what the sign is referring to, in a market scene in a 1922 Stan Laurel film called *The Pest*.

The big purple one in the Quality Street tin gets its shape and size from the Brazil nut, but it no longer actually contains a Brazil nut. It was replaced by the smaller hazelnut in the 1940s. After six years of World War the British public just didn't think they should have to tolerate such a low chocolate to nut ratio any longer. I mean, what were we fighting for...?

So, in summary: Brazil is where the nuts come from. Also, as Brazil happens to be the world leader in transgender surgical procedures, it's where the nuts go, too.

FOOD AND DRINK

Introduction

All the 2014 World Cup games are in the evenings (our time), thanks to a combination of the time difference and FIFA's eagerness to pander to cash-rich European broadcasters with a gluttonous disregard for the players' health and the quality of the actual matches.

This means you will have the perfect opportunity to enhance your enjoyment of the tournament with gastronomic experimentation. To begin with, let's look at ways in which you can get a flavour – literally – of Brazil, the bountiful host nation of this banquet of boot-a-ball.

Now Brazil is such a massive country that there are great regional variations in its cuisine. In the deep South, for example, the gaucho traditions that the region shares with neighbouring Argentina and Uruguay mean that the *churrasco*, a type of meat-heavy barbecue, is very popular. As is heart bypass surgery. The cuisine in Bahia, further up the coast, shows more African influences, while inland and to the North the abundance of forests and freshwater rivers has led to fish and cassava becoming the staple foods.

Let's start with a fish dish, shall we? And what a fish dish it is...

PIRANHA SOUP

Yes, that's right, piranha soup. It's a soup made out of piranha fish, and it comes with the added *frisson* of not knowing whether you are going to eat your dinner or your dinner is going to eat you.

It's worth remembering that the piranha is reputed to be a powerful aphrodisiac, so you might want to prepare this dish on an evening when you are reasonably sure that the match isn't going to go into extra time.

YOU WILL NEED:

Four 2- to 3lb piranha fish
1 big stick (just to be on the safe side)
2 diced carrots
2 bunches of spring onions, chopped green and whites
2 tiny Spanish onions (they are sweeter)
2 hot peppers, diced and seeded
4 steamed and peeled potatoes
3 tomatoes, seeded and chopped
1 tablespoon chopped garlic
8 ounces white wine
2 ounces soy sauce
1 teaspoon turmeric
1 teaspoon toasted ground cumin
1 bunch chopped tarragon
To be very careful...

IMPORTANT TIP:

Do make absolutely sure that your piranha is dead, otherwise warming him up in some soup might just make him perk right up.

Of course, it won't be easy to locate a piranha or two over here on the British high street, four thousand miles from the Amazon basin. It's not the sort of thing you'd normally find in your local Tesco Express – or 'Tescoinho', as they would no doubt style such an establishment in Brazil. Even experienced Amazonian fishermen have trouble landing them, as once one piranha is caught on a hook all his mates start tucking in. And if you catch them in nets, then you have to undertake the ticklish business of disentangling their teeth from the rigging, which can easily cost you a finger.

You may find the best solution for making your

piranha soup is to bung a mackerel or something in there, and then when it is cooked garnish it with a cunningly-positioned set of joke Dracula teeth. For goodness' sake don't cook it with the plastic teeth in; that would probably be horribly toxic.

METHOD:

The piranha fish need to be scaled and gutted, with as many vertical incisions in the skin as possible.

You cook the fish whole, or else chopped into quarters (including the heads, which are the aphrodisiac part).

First sear them in a wide-based pot or a braising pan.

Then remove the fish and add the onions, carrots and garlic, which you sauté until slightly tender. Add the tomatoes and the white wine, and reduce by half before adding the potatoes and soy sauce. Then bung in everything else (apart from the tarragon), including the fish.

Simmer for 20 minutes, season to taste, and add the tarragon. Then your piranha soup is ready. Yum.

Serve in a bowl, then turn on the telly just in time for the kick off of Spain v Chile (or similar).

THE PIRANHA IN FILMS

The piranha has a fearsome reputation. Hunting in lethal shoals, these aggressive and insatiable carnivores can strip the flesh from a cow in seconds, and consequently they have often featured in adventure and horror films. In <u>You Only Live Twice</u>, for example, Bond-nemesis Ernst Stavro Blofeld has an indoor piranha pool in the living room of his volcano-based lair. A couple of people fall in. First the attractive but deadly female who has had sex with Bond and then failed to kill him because the method she chose was needlessly complicated with lots of things that could go wrong. Then the gigantic henchman, the sort of chap that Bond always seems to find himself up against, who can take his best punch without even flinching. On neither occasion do we see any actual individual piranhas munching away, only a sort of ominous underwater bubbling, as though the victims have fallen into a giant Sodastream.

The great B-movie producer Roger Corman made <u>Piranha</u> in 1978 on the back of the Jaws phenomenon, about a genetically-engineered strain of piranhas that were developed as a weapon for the Vietnam War. They end up trying to kill the monsters off using some spare industrial waste.

YOUR DINNER THE STAR

Piranha 3D begins with Richard Dreyfuss, the bloke out of Jaws, playing a bloke a bit like the bloke he played in Jaws. He doesn't want to go on holiday by the sea, of course, on account of the likelihood of being eaten by a shark, so instead he takes a boat out onto a lake in Arizona. There a freak volcanic eruption suddenly releases hundreds of voracious prehistorical piranhas into the lake, all in 3D, which was pretty much the last thing he was expecting, and they all eat him up in double quick time. (Incidentally, I don't know about the piranha's legendary ability to strip the flesh from a cow, but Piranha 3D certainly manages to strip the bikini from Kelly Brook.)

Finally there's Piranhaconda – a fearsome hybrid with the head of a piranha and the body of an anaconda, who has his own little theme tune whenever he looms into view ("Piranha-conda wo-o-o-o-oh!"). Piranhaconda seems just as nimble on the land as in the water, and bites people's heads off with gleeful abandon, before slithering rapidly away without bothering to strip them into skeletons.

Previously in Brazil

The FIFA World Cup has been to Brazil before, in 1950. What follows is a story from then...

The climactic stage of the 1950 tournament was not a knockout with semi-finals and a final, but a four-team round robin between the four group winners: Brazil, Sweden, Spain and Uruguay, the 1930 champions. Brazil won their first two games convincingly, trouncing Sweden 7-1 and Spain 6-1, while Uruguay drew 2-2 with Spain and beat Sweden 3-2. This meant that Brazil only needed to draw with Uruguay in the last match, effectively a final, to lift the trophy.

The Brazilian newspaper *O Mundo* printed a photograph of Brazil on the morning of the game with the caption "These are the World Champions!" Uruguay's captain, Obdulio Varela, bought loads of copies, laid them out on his hotel bathroom floor, and encouraged his team mates to urinate on them.

Later, when the coach made a somewhat defeatist pre-match team talk urging his players to defend as best they could, Varela waited for him to leave and then delivered an emotional speech of his own ending with the memorable injunction "*Muchachos, que empiece la función*" – "Boys, let's start the show!"

An estimated crowd of 210,000, to this day a record for a sports event, packed the Maracana, ready to acclaim their heroes. Brazil duly went into the lead two minutes after half time through Friaça, but goals from Schiaffino and Ghiggia put the underdogs ahead with eleven minutes to go – eleven minutes that were played out in eerie silence.

FIFA president Jules Rimet had prepared a speech in Portuguese for presenting the trophy to Brazil, but in the event there was no presentation ceremony. The Brazilian organisers simply abandoned Rimet on the pitch on his own with the trophy, and he had to wave Varela over so he could give it to him.

The Brazilian Football Confederation had already struck 22 gold winners' medals with the Brazilian squad's names engraved on them, which were hastily put in a drawer somewhere. A song, *Brasil os Vencedores*, had been composed for the occasion, but naturally this was never performed.

Speaking of songs, the renowned football commentator Ary Barroso retired after the game because of the shock and disappointment. Incredibly this was the same Ary Barroso who wrote the iconic song *Aquarelas do Brasil* **(see p.34: World Cup Playlist #1: Songs of Brazil)**, which is a bit like finding out that Motty wrote *Jerusalem*.

Brazil changed the design of their kit after this game, abandoning the white shirts with blue necklines and white shorts because they considered them a jinx. (No, striking 22 gold winners' medals with your names on, *that's* a jinx.) So the iconic yellow shirt emerged from of this debâcle, almost as if to commemorate what happened in Obdulio Varela's bathroom.

The final game of the 1950 World Cup was nicknamed the "Maracanazo", and that became a slang word in Brazil for the triumph of the underdog.

WORLD CUP COLLECTABLES

Panini Stickers

One of the great things about the World Cup coming around is that you can start your own collection of World Cup memorabilia. Of course, it isn't memorabilia yet – not until something has happened to actually be reminded of. Until then your collection is just bilia.

For a kid, collecting can easily become a mini-obsession, which is why starting a collection can be a great way to sneakily get the rest of your family into the World Cup. The daddy of them all is the Panini sticker collection. Panini began producing football stickers in Italy in the 1960s, and brought out their first FIFA World Cup album in 1970. Ever since, the Panini collections have been an essential part of the World Cup landscape.

Of course, you don't have to stick your stickers into the Panini album. They could be used to decorate an exercise book, or a World Cup Wall Chart (**see p.61, 'Pimp Your World Cup Wall Chart'**). No longer bound by the rigid requirements of the album's layout, you could put players alongside one another according to your own criteria. For example, I always used to think Eggen and Chippo would make a tasty midfield combo...

However, if you do want to do it properly, see **'How to Create a World Cup Sticker Album'** on the following spread.

SABAS
PONCE
1970

YOUSSEF
CHIPPO
MAROC

DAN
EGGEN
NORGE

DEUTSCHLAND

STEFAN
KUNTZ

PHILLIP
COCU
NEDERLAND

https://picasaweb.google.com/onlygreatplayers

BRASIL

CARLOS
ALBERTO

ITALIANO

ARGENTINA

DIEGO ARMANDO MARAD

ENGLAND

GORDON
BANKS
1970

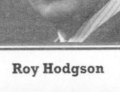

Roy Hodgson

BOBBY
MOORE

HOW TO CREATE A WORLD CUP STICKER ALBUM

1. Buy a World Cup sticker collection album, available in all good shops.

2. Get some packets of the World Cup stickers too. Might as well get quite a few, then you won't have to keep going back. You can drip feed them over the next few weeks. So maybe get twenty packets. No, better make it thirty...

3. When you get home, go into front room and turn off TV/Xbox/PlayStation/Wii so that you have the child or children's full and undivided attention.

4. Present album and stickers to your child or children, saying to your partner: "I used to collect these when I was his (or her) age, I thought he (or she) might get a kick out of it."

5. Accept kudos for this thoughtful gesture.

6. Smile benignly as child (or children) rips open the first packet of stickers with trembling fingers, and spreads them out for inspection.

7. Point out player from obscure country who has funny hair / odd moustache / looks like a serial killer.

8. Also be sure to draw attention to any players whose foreign names are hilariously reminiscent of rude words or parts of the body.

9. Using a small pile of the World Cup stickers, explain the concept of swapsies and "Got Not Got" while riffling through them expertly like a latter-day Paul Daniels.

10. Watch as child attempts to peel the back from their first sticker, trying not to wince as the sticker becomes creased or grubby during this fiddly but formative process.

11. Grimace impatiently as the first couple of stickers go in wonky, before elbowing child/children aside saying "Give me that! You're supposed to get them inside the lines, look, or it will adversely affect the resale value in years to come!"

12. Rip open all thirty packets, and get on with sticking your stickers into your album, maybe with your tongue poking out of one corner of your mouth, ignoring the noise of the TV/Xbox/PlayStation/Wii/iPad/iPod/smartphone, etc.

QUIZ #1

Q1: Gazza's tears captivated a nation when he realised he would be suspended for the World Cup final (actually he was suspended for the third / fourth place play off, as it turned out) after receiving a second booking in the Italia 90 semi-final. Who is the only England player since then to have missed a World Cup finals match because of a suspension?

Q2: Who was England's captain at the 1982 World Cup in Spain?

Q3: What would have happened in the 1966 World Cup Final between England and West Germany had the score remained 2-2 after extra time?

Q4: Under which name did Indonesia become the first Asian country to compete at a World Cup finals, in 1938?

Q5: When it rained on the day of the 1954 World Cup final the West German team had the advantage of exchangeable studs provided by their supplier Adolf Dassler. What was the name of the sporting goods company he founded?

Q6: Which World Cup was the first to be broadcast in colour?

Q7: Which seven English players have missed penalties in shootouts after extra time in World Cup matches?

Q8: What was the name of Scotland's World Cup song in 1998?

Q9: Which player scored in the 1954 final for Hungary, and then represented Spain at the 1962 World Cup in Chile?

Q10: Which two brothers played on opposing teams at the 2010 World Cup?

Q11: Which bald Nosferatu lookalike refereed the 2002 World Cup final in Yokohama?

Q12: Who was England's number 3 at the 1982 World Cup?

Q13: Why did arguably the best side of the 1930s, the Austrian 'wunder' team, withdraw from the 1938 World Cup?

Q14: Where did the World Cup trophy spend the Second World War?

Q15: In which city was the first World Cup finals game played indoors, which is to say under a roof?

Q16: Three of the venues used for the 1966 World Cup in England have since been demolished – which three?

Q17: Which seven players have been members of an England World Cup finals squad whilst belonging to a club outside the UK?

Q18: What was the name of the German goalkeeper who grabbed Frank Lampard's shot from way behind the goal line in 2010 and carried on playing, admitting afterwards that he had deliberately conned the officials?

Q19: Brazil's players dedicated their 1994 World Cup win to which recently-deceased Brazilian sportsman?

Q20: Which three Aston Villa players were in Fabio Capello's 2010 World Cup squad?

Answers on p.221

BRAZIL IN FACTS #2
They have an awful lot of coffee

Certainly if Frank Sinatra is to be believed. As he tells us in 'The Coffee Song':

> *Way down among Brazilians*
> *Coffee beans grow by the billions...*

And who else but Frank would attempt to rhyme 'cherry soda' with 'quota'?

Brazil is the largest producer of coffee in the world, with its 220,000 coffee farms responsible for roughly a third of global output.

You may well be glad of a *café com leite* or two before the World Cup is through, given the lateness of some of the kick-offs, and the achingly tedious slow-slow style of play required to survive in the stifling heat of some of the inappropriately chosen venues closest to the Equator. A good strong injection of *café do Brasil* may be all that keeps you from waking up to find that Gary Lineker has turned into Lorraine Kelly...

CREATE A WORLD CUP PLAYLIST

The World Cup is a chance for musicians to connect with the mass global audience attracted by the bright lights and loud noises of a top international tournament. As a result a four-yearly cycle has sprung up, akin maybe to the so-called "Race for the Christmas Number One", in which a surprising array of artists fall over themselves to have a crack at a World Cup song. I suppose we should be thankful that Cliff only likes tennis.

Music is well known for its uncanny ability to transport you back to a previous state of mind. So a good way to recreate your state of feverish excitement during previous feverishly exciting World Cups (and get you in the mood for this one) would be to put together a World Cup playlist.

Obviously you will want to make your playlist your own, but here are some suggestions for songs you should definitely include, ones you might want to consider, and ones you should definitely avoid...

Key

●●●●● MUST HAVE

●●●● ALMOST ESSENTIAL

●●● MIGHT WANT TO CONSIDER

●● IF YOU LIKE THAT SORT OF THING

✪ ONE TO PIPE INTO THE GERMAN DRESSING ROOM

WORLD CUP PLAYLIST #1
Songs of Brazil

Here are some songs that might help you get into the mood for a Brazilian football fiesta – a bit of samba, a bit of bossa nova, a bit of sunshine, and the vision of a beautiful bronzed girl walking to the beach. We'll get to the football later...

⬤ ⬤ ⬤ ⬤ ⬤ *Mas Que Nada* – Sergio Mendes & Brasil 66

I wouldn't like to bet against hearing an awful lot of this during the World Cup. It is catchy as hell, it says "Brazil" like no other song, and there is a subliminal football link, as it was used to accompany that advert during France 98 where world football stars (including original Ronaldo) booted a ball effortlessly around an airport.

Nike used a version by Tamba Trio for that 1998 ad campaign, but the real iconic version is by Sérgio Mendes, a Brazilian samba icon, and his band Brasil 66. At the time giving the band that name must have felt bang up to date, but the problem is it has a certain built-in obsolescence. Sérgio himself seemed to realise this, and by 1977 the band were called Brasil 77. Then in 1978 Sérgio decided they should be called Brasil 88, losing the plot altogether. It was as if he had suddenly given in to utopian visions of a future in which everyone would samba in their glass-domed cities on the moon.

In Brazilian Portuguese slang, the title *Mas que Nada* literally means "but that's nothing", and carries the sense of "no way", or maybe "whatever", or "Yeah, right!"

Sérgio recorded a version with the Black Eyed Peas which you may like better. But I like the original, and I've a feeling one way or another it's going to be the theme music for whichever television station bagsies it first.

⬤ ⬤ ⬤ ⬤ *The Girl From Ipanema* – Astrud Gilberto, João Gilberto and Stan Getz

Tall and tan and young and lovely, the girl from Ipanema is a symbolic vision of Brazilian beauty.

The song has been recorded many times – indeed it is reputed to be the second most covered song of all, beaten only by *Yesterday* – and it may be you like the version that Amy Winehouse scatted all over, or the one where Frank Sinatra managed to make each admiring "Ooooh!" last halfway into the next line.

However, the classic recording that became an international hit in 1964 was performed by Astrud Gilberto. Her husband, Joao, Stan Getz and composer Antonio Carlos Jobim decided to lay down an English-language version of their Brazilian-Portuguese hit, and Astrud was the only one present who spoke English well so she got the gig. She was not a trained singer, so her version is simple, naïve almost, without any fancy mannerisms or extra twiddles, and it suits the song beautifully.

Interestingly there was an actual girl from Ipanema, a fashionable seaside part of Rio de Janeiro, and each day she did walk to the sea past a café where the song's composers used to drink coffee and await inspiration. Her name is Hélo Pinheiro, and she (naturally) used the song's title as the name of a boutique, whereupon the composers' sons sued her for copyright infringement – and lost.

●●●● *Aquarela do Brasil* – Gal Costa

This is the song known around the world as *Brazil*. Its original title translates as 'Watercolour of Brazil', and it was written in 1939 by Ary Barroso on a night when he was obliged to stay in because of the rain. Barroso said that he wanted to "free the samba from the tragedies of life", and with this song he created a new sub-genre called *samba-exalta*ção, or exaltation samba, joyfully extolling the qualities of his country and people.

The original recording was by Francisco Alves, all muted trumpets and r-r-rolled 'R's, but there are multiple versions. Frank Sinatra (again) mangled it on *Come Fly With Me*, and other artists such as Dionne Warwick seem determined to find the very melancholy that the writer claimed he was trying to escape from.

However, the 1980 version by Gal Costa is bright and bouncy, and will have you playing your mime maracas on the Tube.

●●● *Águas de Março* – Elis and Tom

This is a classic 1974 recording by iconic Brazilian vocalist Elis Regina and composer Tom Jobim. The title means "Waters of March", and describes the rainy season at the end of summer – March being the start of autumn in the Southern hemisphere, of course – with the water bringing and representing birth and rebirth.

The two of them sing to (and over) each other in a clever and sophisticated cat-and-mouse style that feels effortless, almost as though they are making it up as they go along, and the fact that they left in parts of the performance where Elis almost bursts out laughing make this one of the most relaxed and enjoyable listens you could wish for. The song is held in great affection by Brazilians, a vast proportion of whom will have this tucked away in their record collection somewhere.

◉ ◉ *The Coffee Song* – Frank Sinatra

Otherwise known by its hook line, which goes: "They've got an awful lot of coffee in Brazil". Frankie has missed out a couple of times on this playlist, so I thought I'd toss Ol' Blue Eyes a bone. This goofy novelty hit plays on the fact that there is a surplus of coffee in Brazil, so they have to find ways to get rid of the stuff (see p.32).

✪ *Brazil* – Bebi Dol

Don't whatever you do get this one by mistake. This was Yugoslavia's entry to the 1991 Eurovision Song Contest, performed by a sorrowful-looking over-made-up female soloist in Serbian-Croatian-Bosnian. This last-ditch attempt to unify her country proved in vain, as she scored just *un point* and finished next to last, while Yugoslavia began to fragment shortly afterwards. Possibly in shame.

WORLD CUP I-SPY
I-Spy, with my little eye...

Ah, remember the old I-SPY books? Little pocket-sized volumes full of tick boxes?

The idea was to distract young nippers from violence, vandalism and a life of crime (or just from irritating their parents on long car journeys) by encouraging them to keep their eyes peeled for things they could tick off in their I-SPY book. There was an I-SPY book for every possible youthful obsession (i.e. cars, lorries, trains, planes, nature, and Ancient Britain).

So, in the same spirit, here are some things to look out for during the World Cup, along with a points system for those who don't enjoy games without a winner.

1. Television pictures of scantily-clad Brazilian babes dancing in the crowd

This is obviously going to happen a lot, so no points for spotting it on its own. However, if the director is so busy showing us samba-style babes that we miss something important on the pitch, there are definitely points available for that, as follows:

If you find yourself watching said babes, then return to the action in time for a free kick, but haven't seen the offence for which the kick was given – **5 points** ☐

If you return to see a player walking off the field, red carded, but have no earthly idea why – **10 points** ☐

If you miss a goal – you scoff but I bet it is going to happen at least once – **50 points**

If you see a samba-style babe with a massive headdress cavorting around trying to attract the cameraman's eye, while behind her a grumpy-looking chap shifts from side to side trying to see the game – **20 points**

BONUS If the director lingers lasciviously over a gyrating *senhorita*, yet it becomes incontrovertibly clear that the *senhorita* is really a *senhor* – **100 points**

2. Sepp Blatter gets something wrong

This will be very easy to spot, as the man can barely open his mouth without ramming his feet in there.

At the draw ceremony there was a minute's silence to honour the just-departed Nelson Mandela. After ten seconds, Sepp Blatter unilaterally decided that this should be a minute's applause. That is the sort of fellow we are dealing with here. So:

Sepp undermines a ref's decision – **5 points**

Sepp calls for new technology to be introduced, even though he has been its main opponent – **15 points**

Sepp gets something else wrong – **25 points**

3. Luis Suarez handles the ball

Illegally that is, rather than just before kick-off, or posing for the team photograph, or taking a throw in, or if the Uruguay goalkeeper gets sent off and they've used all their subs so he goes in goal like used to happen in the olden days. No, I mean when he handles it in open play, then tries to carry on as if nothing untoward has happened...

A free kick is awarded – **5 POINTS.**

He gets away with it scot free – **15 POINTS.**

He does it in such a way that it knocks England out of the tournament (statistically possible) – actually only **7 POINTS.** Somehow it doesn't seem that unlikely...

4. Commentator or ex-player pundit says something that doesn't make any sense at all

For instance: "The team equipped themselves well." You hear this one all the time. Rather than acquitted. It's just possible the speaker means they tied their boots on really neatly, or got their shinpads the right way round. But I don't think so.

During Euro 96 the eminent Barry Davies said of a burly German midfield stopper: "There's Dieter Eilts, built like a brick door!" Now clearly there is no such thing as a brick door – what would be the point of it? What Barry's done here, I reckon, is he's got stuck between two well-known similes – "built like a brick shithouse" and "bangs like a shithouse door". His über-professional broadcasting instincts have told him, midway through the first of these, that you simply can't use the word "shithouse" on the BBC, and so he has suddenly changed course, unfortunately towards the other popular shithouse-related simile, thereby generating a whole new piece of nonsense for posterity.

Glenn Hoddle is good for this sort of thing, too. I recently heard him describe a bit of skilful play – by Ross Barkley, as it happens – as "delineous". What was he going for there, I wonder? Delicious, perhaps? Delirious? Delineated?

Any suitable example by a commentator (remember, they are *in extremis*) – **5 POINTS** ☐

Any suitable example by a pundit (who has more time to think) – **10 POINTS** ☐

Unless it's Robbie Savage, in which case – **1 POINT** ☐

CASUAL DEFENDING

5. "SLOPPY", "CASUAL" & "NAIVE"

It's like there was a memo to all football pundits saying don't use the word 'BAD'. Alan Hansen probably protested: "You're joking! What, not even in the phrase 'that was rank bad defending'?!" But the ban came down from on high, so alternatives had to be found.

When pundits say '**SLOPPY**' they mean 'bad'. (When Alan Hansen says '*slorpy*' he means 'sloppy'). Sloppy is everywhere now. Any mistake, a slip, a stumble, a miskick – *oh, that's just sloppy.*

Then there's **CASUAL**. *Oh, that's casual.* When pundits say 'casual' they mean 'bad'. Sometimes a player can be 'too casual'. He was too casual with that pass – as if it was all right to attempt to play that particular ball, only not wearing slacks, sipping a Campari and leaning against a mantelpiece by a roaring fire.

Finally we come to **NAIVE**. Naïvety is a quality of innocence; a lack of experience or sophistication. When pundits say 'naïve' they mean 'bad'. It sounds odd when they use it to describe defending, as though a centre half had never imagined that an opposing forward might use skill to confound him. Of all things....

For each **SLOPPY**, **CASUAL** or **NAÏVE** you hear, award yourself **3 POINTS**

WORLD CUP SKILLS #2

The Scorpion

Strictly speaking, this is not a World Cup Skill (not yet anyway – fingers crossed), but René Higuita, the Colombian goalkeeper who first demonstrated it, was certainly a man with World Cup previous. Indeed, he pretty much needed to develop something as spectacular as the Scorpion to avoid forever being remembered as the goalkeeper who ridiculously tried to out-dribble Cameroon's Roger Milla on the edge of the centre circle at Italia 90, leaving the veteran striker the freedom of a whole half of the pitch to score the winner.

Higuita was already bidding to make a lasting mark with his eye-catching hairdo, a mop of black ringlets, but when you come from the country that produced Carlos Valderrama you are really up against it.

So during a Wembley friendly against England in 1995 Higuita unveiled the Scorpion that became his trademark, and his alone.

After a bit of penalty area ping-pong, and some momentary confusion over whether an offside had been given, the ball came to Jamie "wivart-a-dart" Redknapp. He lofted the ball goalwards, and it was clearly going to drop over Higuita and into the net unless he did something about it. Like just reaching his hands up into the air and catching it, as per page one of the goalie handbook. Perhaps worried that some stray mud might fall from the ball into his wet-look ringlets, or else in that moment mindful of his place in history, the Colombian suddenly pitched himself forwards, and flung his legs up high into the air behind himself to bash the ball clear with his heels. The football world gasped – and a reputation was made.

FOOD AND DRINK

Churrasco

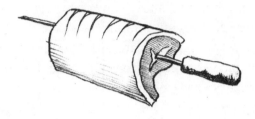

In the olden days gauchos herded cattle all over the pampas of Southern Brazil, Uruguay and Northern Argentina. Naturally enough, since they were looking at it all day long, they developed a meat-based cuisine, which you too can enjoy – though you may not want to prepare your cuts of meat in quite the same way. The old cattle herders used a trick they had borrowed from the Indians, and laid raw meat across their horses' backs as they rode along. Then, at *churrasco* time, the meat would be naturally seasoned by the horse's sweat, and ready to be cooked. Gack...

The *churrasco* style of cooking involved a fire pit surrounded by long skewers of meat stuck in the ground, which would be turned periodically to cook the meat evenly. Basically it was a great big barbecue, and that is what it has become nowadays for the modern Brazilian. If you'd rather not dig a fire hole in your lawn, you can buy a *churrasqueira* to do the job, which is a barbecue grill with supports for the spits.

Or you can head out to a *churrascaria*, a restaurant serving barbecue-grilled meats. Usually the food is served by waiters carrying the skewers like swords. They then slice the meat directly onto your plate, in a style known as *rodízio*. Often these are all-you-can-eat establishments, and you are provided with a little paddle with a green side and a red side to wave in the air so you can indicate either your readiness for further face-stuffing (green) or the completion of that process (red) without having to interrupt your chewing by speech.

So how to make your British summer garden barbecue into a proper *churrasco*?

Well, perhaps unsurprisingly, it's all about the meat. Make sure you procure the right cuts of meat.

The *picanha* is a cut of beef highly favoured in Brazil. It translates as the 'rump cap', and is usually covered in a thick layer of fat, which is left on for cooking.

Another is the *fraldinha*, which is a long flat flank steak – actually the stuff Lady Gaga used for her meat dress, if you are interested in fashion. Or meat.

A Brazilian *churrasco* will also feature plenty of chicken and sausage like the *linguiça calabrese*, a spicy Italian variety.

So: squirt some start-up juice on the charcoal, keep the giant skewers away from the kids, and have yourself a meat party, Brazilian-style.

NOTE: in Argentina and Uruguay, gauchos would top up their cholesterol by popping a fried egg on top of their *churrasco*. Not strictly a Brazilian thing, but I can't see how that is possibly going to make it worse...

WORLD CUP COLLECTABLES

Forecourt Freebies

Esso gave us the first great petrol station collectables. The 1970 World Cup Coin Collection was captivating for kids, who suddenly began begging to be taken on long drives to visit old and boring relatives in the hope that Dad would have to fill up in an Esso garage.

Each coin – I say coin, they made an unimpressive plasticky noise if you dropped them – featured the head of an England squad member, and there were 30 of them, so it was fiendishly hard to collect them all.

Esso didn't venture another World Cup coin collection until 1990, when they produced slightly more metallic coins of both the England and Scotland squads.

In 1998 BP brought out little cartoon cards of the England squad, which were OK, but didn't jingle satisfyingly in the pocket. It felt like an opportunity missed, and with that sort of muddled thinking the Deepwater Horizon disaster just twelve short years later was hardly a surprise.

The coin collecting mantle passed to Sainsbury's for the 1998 World Cup (not strictly speaking a petrol company, but they do have petrol stations). Uniquely, they went to the trouble of bringing out extra coins to cover their mistaken picks when the actual squad was announced, which was thoughtful, and makes the whole thing into a more historically accurate artefact.

The next give-away-with-fuel offering was from

Texaco, who went out on a limb and produced 'pogs' for 2006. Pogs were round laminated discs that were a game-craze in the 1990s. You would slam one of your pogs at a pile of somebody else's, and keep any that landed face up. The game was banned in many schools because it seemed to resemble gambling.

Even stranger than pogs were Esso's 2010 offerings. These were called medallions, but in fact were thick, square, laminated cardboard objects that resembled miniature coasters – maybe something you could use to protect your table top from a shot glass, or a small biscuit, but nothing much larger.

We don't yet know if any petrol giants will take the plunge in 2014, but hopefully we will see a return to proper coins with barely recognisable reliefs of players' faces and tiny etched autographs. Textbook.

*** BONUS ASTRONOMY FEATURE ***

The Night Sky

As mentioned in the Health and Safety warning, a month is a long time to just sit on the sofa watching football, and you really should take every opportunity to get up, stretch your legs and go outside. Perhaps you are already taking advantage of some of the suggestions for World Cup skills you can practise in your garden or local park.

However, this year's tournament has been scheduled in such a way that some of the games are well after dark, at an hour when it is no longer practical to be attempting the Blanco Hop, so this chapter will point out some features of the night sky that you can pop out into your garden and look for, thus both stretching your legs and getting fresh air.

Since time immemorial the ancients have discerned bewitching patterns in the night sky, representing heroic characters and memorable incidents from their myths and legends, so why shouldn't we do the same in the 21st century? After all, new stars are being discovered all the time, and surely the heavens have room for myths both ancient and modern.

So, here are some constellations for you to look for as you wait for the second half of that 2am kick off in Recife.

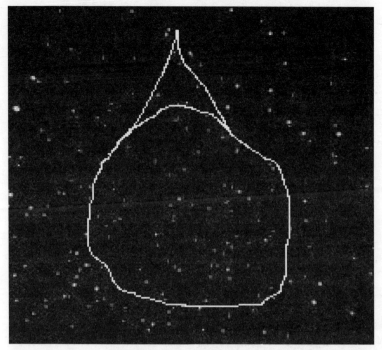

Fig 1. As you look East you can quite clearly discern this constellation, which is in the shape of David Beckham's hairdo from the 2002 World Cup. in Japan.

Fig 2. This is a nice clear image of Chris Waddle's penalty kick from the semi-final of Italia 90. It comes around every 24 years, having carved an elliptical path through the asteroid belt.

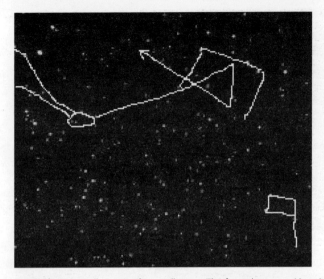

Fig 3. This is actually a pair of constellations. The first is known as **Hurst's Lucky Goal** – you should be able to make out Sir Geoff's outstretched leg and boot, steering the ball against the crossbar, down (clearly over the line) and out again. To the right is the smaller constellation, **The Russian Linesman's Flag**.

Fig 4. Here, as visible as the Plough or Orion The Parallelogram-Shaped Hunter, is the twin feature **Zidane-Materazzi**, which uncannily captures the moment the French genius nutted his Italian tormentor in the chest.

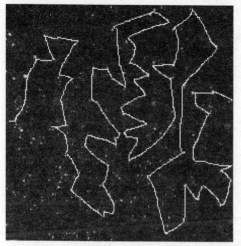

Fig 5. The Spanish Attack. A heavenly view of the football played by the victorious Spanish in the 2010 World Cup Final. We can clearly see the ball being rolled out by keeper Iker Casillas to his left full back, then a prolonged period of intricate passing follows, which in fact lasted 4.5 minutes, before Fernando Torres scuffs it into the hands of the Dutch keeper.

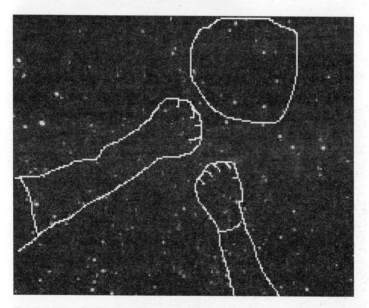

Fig 6. Mano de Dios, la Mano de Shilton. All the great constellations tell a story, and the tale told here is one of perfidy unpunished, of a cheat who prospered, and of a tragic Tunisian referee who never officiated again. Fortunately only visible in the Southern hemisphere.

Keep watching the skies!

THE ULTIMATE WORLD CUP WALL CHART

You have to have a World Cup wall chart.

No discussion. No prevarication. No backsliding.

In *An Evening With Gary Lineker* (a football play I wrote with Arthur Smith about some people watching the Italia 90 semi-final in a Majorca hotel) the wife of a football fan gets so cheesed off with her husband's obsession that she sets fire to his World Cup wall chart. Does this put him off? Well no, as the wife explains:

"Annoyingly he was actually quite pleased to have to do it all over again."

So a proper wall chart is absolutely key to your enjoyment of the World Cup. If you have kids, then this can be an important and enjoyable way to spark their enthusiasm, as well as providing a fun activity you can do together (as long as you can restrain yourself from shouting "No! No! Not like that! You're going over the edges! Give me the pencils! Give them to me! And the glue, come on! Now sit over there and be quiet...!")

In the area of World Cup wall chart creation and acquisition there are various routes open to you.

One: get a wall chart from out of a newspaper.
Really? That's what you're going to do? They are liable to be very small and fiddly, you know, with teeny tiny boxes for the scores, and no room to put in goal scorers. And without the rest of the paper to back it up there's

a good chance of your biro going straight through it like a thumbnail through toilet paper (and nobody wants that). The most important consideration is this. No one is going to come round your house and admire your World Cup wall chart if you've just sellotaped a puny pull-out from the paper to your wall. So sort yourself out.

Two: get a gigantic piece of paper and DIY-it-yourself.

At the other end of the spectrum there is getting a gigantic piece of paper, a load of coloured pencils, a ruler, and a gung-ho go-get-'em attitude. I applaud this approach, and believe that you and your child may find this a most rewarding and enjoyable bonding experience. I would not want to deter you from doing this, not for one moment.

If, however, that seems like a lot of work (and it is, there's a *load* of measuring to do for starters) then maybe you will allow me to help out...

Three: simply follow the instructions overleaf.

HOW TO MAKE A WORLD CUP WALL CHART FROM THE THINGS THAT ARE CUNNINGLY PROVIDED WITHIN THIS BOOK YOU HAVE ALREADY BOUGHT.

See? Extra value. This book is practically paying for itself. OK, so it may be a bit like something out of a *Blue Peter* annual, but we can live with that, can't we?

YOU WILL NEED:

- A sheet of A2 paper (could be white, but doesn't have to be). As Lesley Judd might have said, blithely unaware of her *double entendres*: "Best if it is quite stiff…"

- Scissors (don't run with these, kids)

- Glue (don't sniff this, kids) or a Pritt stick (other brands of things that are a bit like a Pritt stick are available)

- Paper (watch out for those paper cuts, kids)

- Coloured pencils, pens or crayons (don't see how many you can get in your sister's nose, kids)

- Sticky-back plastic and an old squeezy bottle (not allowed to say Fairy Liquid), two coat hangers, and some tinsel… Oh no, not tinsel, hang on, this is only for if you want to make the *Blue Peter* advent crown. Move on.

- Computer with printer attached (do not try to eat this, kids, or suck the ink out of the printer cartridges)

- A razor-sharp art scalpel or Stanley knife (don't even take this out of the packet, kids, put it in a drawer or in Dad's toolbox, and forget I ever mentioned it).

- This book, the one in your hand now.

INSTRUCTIONS

OK. In the next section of the book you will find a chapter on each of the eight groups in the first phase of the tournament. These sections begin with a block showing the FIXTURES for each group, and these eight blocks are the first thing you will need.

You can either:
- Photocopy these pages, then cut out the fixture blocks.
- Scan these pages, and then print them out and cut out the fixture blocks.
- Cut them out of the book. (Although this will pretty much ruin the book, meaning you have to buy another one...)

Or:
- Download them from the 'Wall Chart' section of the website and print them out.

Then for each group you will also need a GROUP TABLE. We have included a template for these (overleaf), which you can either:
- Photocopy (eight times) and then cut out the group table templates.
- Scan and print out (eight times) and then cut out the group table templates.

Or:
- Download the template from the 'Wall Chart' section of the website and print them out.

		W	D	L	F	A	Pts
	✂						
	✂						
	✂						

So now you should have your eight blocks of fixtures for Groups A to H, and your eight blank group table templates.

- Take your A2 sheet, and draw a line across it 24 cm from the top.
- Stick four of your group tables along this line, and then stick the fixtures for Groups A to D above that.
- Then stick the fixture blocks for Groups E to H below the line, and the four remaining group tables below that.

This takes care of the first phase of the tournament.

Then there are three more pages for you to copy/scan/cut out/download, which are the fixture page for the Second Round, the one for the Quarter Finals, and the page containing the Semi Finals and Final (see p.142).

There should be room aplenty on the bottom part of the wall chart for you to paste these alongside each other, or in whatever jaunty fashion you fancy. Then there will be more space for you to stick other fascinating and colourful stuff, around the bottom and across the top (see section, 'Now Pimp Your Wall Chart').

As things stand, your World Cup wall chart-in-progress will be a strictly monochrome affair, which may suit your home, but if not, or if you are a little more ambitious, well, you have two choices.

- **One**: you (and your child/children) can get cracking with the old coloured pencils.
- **Two**: you can go to **the *How To Enjoy The World Cup* website** – www.howtoenjoytheworldcup.net

There you can download coloured labels for each team, to be printed out and inserted into the appropriate Second Round/Quarter Final/etc places when/if those teams progress in the tournament. Paste them at the top of the relevant box, and you will leave yourself just enough room to write goalscorers in underneath. You'll see what I mean.

As I've already mentioned, from the website you can also download the Group Fixture and Table pages, already in glorious Technicolor...

BONUS FEATURE: You can also download league tabs for each team. Remember when *Shoot!* used to do those league ladders? With the little cardboard tabs you could switch around to keep up to date with the league table throughout the season? Well, this is the same idea as that. Because the drawback with most – nay, I will go so far as to say *all* – other World Cup wall charts is that there is really no point in filling in the Group Tables until the group matches are all over, but with Team Tabs you can show the current state of each group throughout the first phase.

So download and print the 32 coloured tabs from the website – on thick paper or card, if you want to do it properly – and cut them all out. Then with some pointy scissors (or possibly a blade or sharp knife, if that's more your kind of thing), cut out the slots as marked on the Group Tables, and slot the tabs home. You'll get the hang of it – if not, there might be a Helpline, if we can be bothered to set one up, or maybe the bloke in A&E when you show him how you sliced the tip of your finger off will be able to give you some pointers...

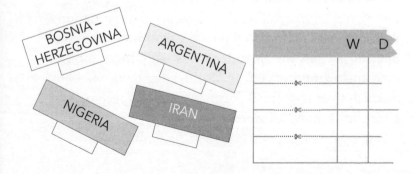

NOW PIMP YOUR WALL CHART

So that's the basics taken care of.

Now it's time to pimp the thing within an inch of its life!

To begin with, take a look at the bits and pieces you can download from our website (see back cover).

Or from the internet generally (then we don't have to even think about the various copyright ramifications, which would probably be a good thing).

Your wallchart can thus be as up-to-date as you could possibly want, unlike that one you got out of the *Guardian*, which is far too tiny and has photographs from 2010 on it (I'm guessing).

How about bringing the fairy lights down from the loft?

Why not decorate with spare stickers from your Panini collection?

Sequins. Sequins are always classy.

Or you could add some special opening windows with chocolate behind them like an advent calendar. Offhand I can't think how you might actually do this, but if you pull it off kudos to you – and your kids will love you. (The daughter of a friend of mine has devised an advent calendar style wall chart for the next tournament to cover all the qualifying matches as well, meaning she'll get a constant supply of free chocolate for two years).

Mag wheels (may not be practical in all cases).

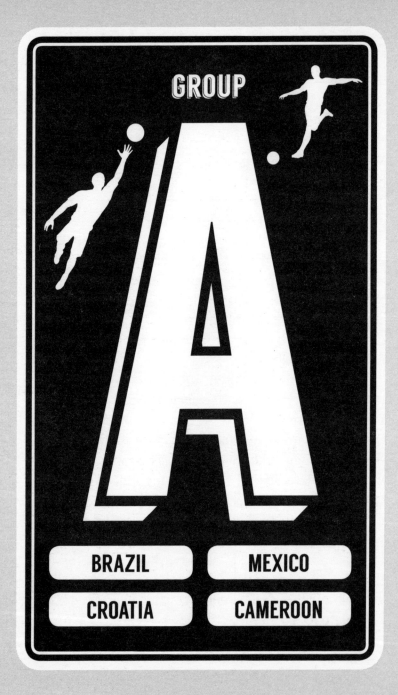

GROUP

A

| BRAZIL | MEXICO |
| CROATIA | CAMEROON |

GROUP A

12 JUNE	21:00 ITV			SAO PAULO
BRAZIL				CROATIA

13 JUNE	17:00 ITV			NATAL
MEXICO				CAMEROON

17 JUNE	20:00 BBC			FORTALEZA
BRAZIL				MEXICO

18 JUNE	23:00 ITV			MANAUS
CAMEROON				CROATIA

23 JUNE	21:00 ITV			BRASILIA
CAMEROON				BRAZIL

23 JUNE	21:00 ITV			RECIFE
CROATIA				MEXICO

	W	D	L	F	A	Pts

BRAZIL

FIFA RANKING: 10   World cup wins: 5

Kit: The Classic – yellow shirts with green trim, blue shorts, white socks

World cup odds: 3-1 (1st favourites)

BRA

NOT ONLY THE LARGEST COUNTRY IN SOUTH AMERICA, it takes up nearly half of the continent. Brazil is the fifth largest country in the world, both by area and population, and is significantly better at football than any of the ones that are bigger than them on either list. Their FIFA ranking has suffered in the last couple of years because they have not needed to play qualifying games, but their convincing triumph at last year's Confederations Cup shows that that they are still the major force in the world game and justifiably massive favourites.

How they got there:

They persuaded Sepp Blatter that it was high time for another South American World Cup, and promised they could attract billions of dollars of private investment, produce state-of-the-art new stadia, and finish some much-vaunted infrastructure projects. Not sure how that's all going...

How will they do?

Well, put it this way; if they don't win it in style 200 million tear-stained fans are going to want to know the reason why. They could be seriously tested fairly early, with one or other of the 2010 finalists lying in wait in the first knockout game. Having their party pooped at that stage hardly bears thinking about...

The Manager:

Big Phil Scolari guided Brazil to the title in 2002, which should settle home fans' nerves. He was also, however, in charge of the Portugal team that lost to Greece in the final of Euro 2004, which should keep them up nights.

Watch out for:

Much will be expected of 22-year-old Neymar. He will wear the number 10, like Pele, and started out at Santos, the master's old club, before moving to Barcelona last summer. The willowy trickster was named best player as Brazil won the Confederations Cup. If Brazil use him as their main creator, then it could be Fred of Fluminense who is responsible for actually banging the goals in.

Premiership Pals:

Paulinho of Spurs should join Oscar, Ramires, Willian and Sideshow Bob of Chelsea. Júlio César, out of favour and game time at QPR, has been promised a place in the squad too, and Liverpool's Lucas may have a chance. Robinho, Jô and Anderson are possible ex-Premiership faces who could figure as well.

World Cup Previous:

No nation has more World Cup previous than Brazil, who have lifted the trophy five times. They won in Sweden in 1958, inspired by the teenage Pele, and again in Chile four years later. Their 4-1 triumph against Italy in the 1970 final is probably the most fondly-remembered of all World Cup matches. A sun-baked shoot out brought them the prize again in Pasadena in 1994, while two-goal Ronaldo saw off the Germans in 2002. In addition they have been runners up twice, in 1950 and 1998, and third twice, in 1938 and 1978. Beat that.

CAMEROON

CMR

FIFA RANKING: 59 World cup wins: 0
Kit: Green shirts (with sleeves, this time), red shorts, yellow socks.
World cup odds: 750-1 (=27th favourites)

C AMEROON IS SITUATED ON THE GULF OF GUINEA, JUST where the African coast stops going west-east, turns right, and starts going north-south. The country is known as "Africa in miniature", because it has all the major climates, vegetations and geographical features of the continent – coast, desert, mountains, savanna and rainforest. In 2002 their football team sported a basketball-style sleeveless vest, which FIFA banned from the World Cup. Then in 2004 they introduced a one-piece kit like a leotard, which FIFA declared illegal despite there being nothing in their own rules about it.

How they got there:

The Indomitable Lions topped their qualifying group, ahead of Libya, Congo DR and Togo, and then overcame Tunisia in a two-legged play-off. A goalless first leg was followed by an emphatic 4-1 win in the home leg in Yaoundé, with two goals from Jean Makoun.

How will they do?

They could turn Mexico over, and may enjoy playing in Manaus more than Croatia will, so they have a chance at least of finishing second in the group. It's hard to see them emulating their 1990 heroics, though.

The Manager:

Nobody has held onto the job for very long in recent times, and the current incumbent is a suspiciously blonde 65-year-old German called Volker Finke, with 16 years as coach of SC Freiburg behind him and no experience of the African football scene at all.

Watch out for:

There are few better spotters of footballing horseflesh than Arsene Wenger (if you ignore the occasional Igor Stepanovs). He snapped up a promising 17-year-old called Alex Song in 2005 and developed him into one of the top all-action midfielders in the world, who now struts his stuff for Barcelona. I am also hoping that Gaetan Bong has a good shot on him, as a Partridge-esque commentatorial cry of "Bong!!!" would be a joy, wouldn't it?

Premiership Pals:

Chelsea's Samuel Eto'o is the captain. Sebastian Bassong of Norwich and Benoit Assou-Ekotto, once Spurs, now QPR, should also be familiar, as should former Gunner Alex Song. Jean Makoun didn't pull up any trees at Aston Villa. One-time Old Trafford misfit Djemba-Djemba has set his sights on a comeback, now that he is a Premiership player once again. Scottish Premiership, that is, with St Mirren. Good luck with that.

World Cup Previous:

Cameroon's finest World Cup moments were at Italia 90, where they beat defending champions Argentina in the opening game, and went on a run to the quarter final, where they took England to extra time before finally succumbing to a couple of Gary Lineker penalties. Otherwise they have not got past the group stage in five other attempts, unlucky and unbeaten in 1982, undistinguished in 1994, 1998, 2002 and in 2010, when they were the very first team to be knocked out.

CROATIA

FIFA RANKING: 16   World cup wins: 0

Kit: Distinctive red and white checkerboard shirts, white shorts, blue socks.

World cup odds: 150-1 (=20th favourites)

CRO

B EFORE CROATIA BECAME AN INDEPENDENT COUNTRY in 1991 and joined FIFA and UEFA in its own right the following year, Croatian footballers played for the Kingdom of Yugoslavia (1919-39) and the Socialist Federal Republic of Yugoslavia (1945-90). They were fortunate to have a so-called Golden Generation to establish them as a force in European football straight away, with players like Boban, Prosinečki, Bilić, Jarni and Šuker making a strong showing at both Euro 96 and France 98. Since then the highlights have been fewer and further between, but they did end the England career of the Wally with the Brolly in 2007.

How they got there:

Croatia took second place in their group behind runaway leaders Belgium, managing to stay ahead of Serbia despite losing three of their last four games, including two defeats by Scotland. Iceland fancied their chances against them in the play offs, but Croatia managed to squeak past them 2-0 on aggregate.

How will they do?

Under Slaven Bilić, Croatia had a decent Euro 2012, only losing narrowly to Spain. Since then, however, they have gone into a bit of a slump, and they could struggle to make much of an impression on Group A.

The Manager:

Niko Kovac, at 42, is one of the youngest coaches at the World Cup, and was still playing as Croatia's captain only six years ago. Has a reputation as a good motivator, but may be found out tactically.

Watch out for:

It's not much to cling to, considering they are in a group with Brazil, but Croatia do have a little bit of home advantage to call on. Eduardo, now second on their all-time scoring list behind Davor Šuker, was actually born in Rio de Janeiro, moving to Dinamo Zagreb as a sixteen year old. His time at Arsenal was blighted by serious injury and diving controversies, and he now plays at Shaktar Donetsk with a lot of other Brazilians and his national team skipper, Darijo Srna.

Premiership Pals:

Dejan Lovren plays centre back for Southampton. Nikica Jelavić moved from Everton to not-Hull-City-Tigers-yet in January. At roughly the same time Mladen Petrić left West Ham for Panathinaikos. Eduardo was a Gunner, Vedran Corluka turned out for Spurs and Man City, and Redknapp-favourite Niko Krancjar of QPR also starred for Portsmouth and Spurs.

World Cup Previous:

There were Croatians in the Yugoslavia team that finished third in 1930. The very first time they were able to compete as an independent nation they also finished third, at France 98. The highlight of their tournament was a 3-0 quarter final defeat of Germany, and they led in the semi-final before two Lilian Thuram goals knocked them out. They didn't get out of the group stage in 2002 (lost to Mexico) or 2006 (lost to Brazil), and didn't qualify at all last time from England's group – remember that Theo Walcott hat-trick.

MEXICO

FIFA RANKING: 20   **World cup wins: 0**
Kit: Green shirts, white shorts, white socks with red tops.
World cup odds: 125-1 (16th favourite)

THERE ARE MORE SPANISH SPEAKERS IN MEXICO THAN in any other country, including Spain, and only Brazil has more Catholics. The Spanish conquistadors brought bullfighting to Mexico, and it is the national sport, even though fútbol is actually more popular. Before the Spanish came, the Aztecs used to play a game called *ollama* on a field or court called a *tlachtli*, in which the participants had to strike a ball through a stone ring fixed to a wall – a bit like that made-up game in Harry Potter, except much more violent, and the losers would be sacrificed to the Sun-god.

How they got there:

Mexico had an unusually torrid time in qualifying. They only won two of their ten CONCACAF qualifiers, and were obliged to tackle a two-legged play off against New Zealand. They won that 9-3 on aggregate, with five of their goals notched by Oribe Peralta.

How will they do?

Despite their unconvincing route to the tournament, Mexico are narrowly favoured to finish second in Group A behind Brazil. They might even fancy their chances of springing a big surprise against the hosts, having pipped them to Olympic gold two years ago. A potential second round game against either Spain or Netherlands could be tricky.

The Manager:

When Miguel Herrera took over back in October he was the fourth Mexican national team coach in a month, and he managed to get their campaign back on track just in the nick of time. Previously he managed América – not the USA national side, but the Mexico City-based club giants.

Watch out for:

Oribe Peralta is a 30-year-old striker, who has played all his club football in his home country, never landing that big-money switch to Europe despite some great stats. He scored both his team's goals in the 2012 Olympic football final at Wembley as Mexico won gold, beating Brazil (Neymar, Oscar, Hulk et al) 2-1, and he averages a goal every other game for the full national team.

Premiership Pals:

Manchester United's Javier "Chicarito" Hernandez, the little pea, is the stand out Premiership Mexican. Giovani dos Santos of Villareal had a spell at Spurs, and was runner-up for the title of Young Player of the 2010 World Cup. Former misfiring-Gunner Carlos Vela decided to let the manager know he was not available because he was "not 100% mentally and emotionally ready". Only polite to do so.

World Cup Previous:

Mexico have qualified for fourteen World Cups, and actually played in the very first World Cup game in 1930 against France. They have reached the quarter finals twice, in 1970 and 1986, the two occasions when they hosted the tournament. They have gone out at the last 16 stage in each of the last five World Cups, on the last two occasions losing to Argentina

GROUP

B

SPAIN
NETHERLANDS
CHILE
AUSTRALIA

GROUP B

13 JUNE	20:00 BBC		SALVADOR
SPAIN			NETHERLANDS

13 JUNE	23:00 ITV		CUIABA
CHILE			AUSTRALIA

18 JUNE	20:00 BBC		RIO DE JANEIRO
SPAIN			CHILE

18 JUNE	17:00 ITV		PORTO ALEGRE
AUSTRALIA			NETHERLANDS

23 JUNE	17:00 ITV		CURITIBA
AUSTRALIA			SPAIN

23 JUNE	17:00 ITV		SAO PAULO
NETHERLANDS			CHILE

	W	D	L	F	A	Pts
........✀........						
........✀........						
........✀........						

73

SPAIN

FIFA RANKING: 1   World cup wins: 1
Kit: Red shirts with yellow trim, blue shorts, red socks.
World cup odds: 7-1 (4th favourites)

ESP

S PAIN'S STAGGERING SUCCESSES IN RECENT YEARS HAVE been built on tiki-taka football. The name derives from a plastic juggling toy such as was faddishly popular in the UK playgrounds of the 1970s, and so translates into English as "clackers", which is pleasing. Tiki-taka tactics require technically gifted footballers who excel at keeping possession for long periods with quick passing and accomplished ball control. When it works it can look unbeatable, but critics such as Arsene Wenger see it as "first and foremost a way not to lose" rather than an attacking philosophy.

How they got there:

Obliged to qualify even though they were the reigning champions, Spain topped European Group I ahead of France. Their away victory at the Stade de France proved crucial, the decisive goal coming from Barcelona's Pedro.

How will they do?

Ordinarily you would really fancy their chances, given that they have won the last three major tournaments in which they have competed. However, they are slow starters, and it looks like they will have to top Group B to avoid meeting Brazil again long before what would be most people's idea of a great final.

The Manager:

Vicente del Bosque is the only man to have managed winning teams in the Champions League (Real Madrid), the European Championships and the World Cup (Spain). After the 2010 victory in South Africa he was made the 1st Marquis of Del Bosque by King Juan Carlos – and to think Alf Ramsey only got a knighthood.

Watch out for:

The first time I remember noticing Andrés Iniesta was in the 2006 Champions League final. Arsenal were clinging onto a 1-0 lead against Barcelona when suddenly the Catalans brought on a substitute who was straightaway the best player on the pitch by a mile. Since then Iniesta has become one of the cornerstones of the national team and arguably its most important player, winning Man of the Match awards in both the finals of Euro 2012 and the 2010 World Cup.

Premiership Pals:

David Silva, Alvaro Negredo and Jésus Navas of Manchester City, Nacho Monreal and Santi Cazorla of Arsenal, David de Gea and Juan Mata of Manchester United, Roberto Soldado of Spurs and Chelsea's Fernando Torres and César Azpilicueta. In addition there'll be plenty of Premiership memories, fond or otherwise, of Xabi Alonso, Pepe Reina and Alvaro Arbeloa at Anfield, of one-time Gunner Cesc Fàbregas, and of former Fergie Fledgling Gerard Piqué.

World Cup Previous:

Until recently, Spain were traditionally the team that never fulfilled their potential. They were fourth in 1950, but apart from that had never got past the quarter finals before triumphantly tiki-taka-ing all the way in 2010. Their best showing was probably in 2002 when they went home unbeaten, having been eliminated on penalties by South Korea.

NETHERLANDS

NED

FIFA RANKING: 8   World cup wins: 0

Kit: All orange, one of the iconic kits of world football.

World cup odds: 28-1 (=9th favourites)

B ACK IN THE 1970S, WHEN CRUYFF AND AJAX RULED European football, the national team used to be known, more often than not, as Holland. Strictly speaking, though – and I'm sure you can hear in your mind's ear Stephen Fry catching Alan Davies out with this one – Holland refers to only two provinces of the Netherlands, North and South Holland, which represent only just over an eighth of the whole country. So the Netherlands is the proper way to refer to the land of tulips and total football, the philosophy which liberated players from fixed positions in rigid tactical systems so that anyone could pop up anywhere.

How they got there:

The Dutch won nine out of ten qualifying games in European Group D and drew the other to complete the most comfortable campaign of all. Robin van Persie scored eleven goals, including a hat trick in the 8-1 demolition of Hungary.

How will they do?

Their opening match against Spain, a re-run of the 2010 final, could decide their fate. Win that and they could top the group, lose it and they could face Brazil in the second round. A draw, though, and it could be total football versus tiki-taka to see who can score the most in the other group matches.

The Manager:

Louis van Gaal is in his second stint in charge, his first having ended with failure to qualify for the 2002 World Cup. Has a reputation for producing vibrant attacking football teams, and for losing his cool with reporters who ask him what he regards as stupid questions.

Watch out for:

Van Gaal took Arjen Robben to Bayern Munich in 2009, and his Champions League trademark since then has been cutting in from the right and smashing in a shot from the edge of the area with his left. The balding maestro is a definite match-winner, but the Netherlands have a few – Wesley Sneijder for one, Rafael van der Vaart for another – and Robin van Persie and Klaas-Jan Huntelaar should bring them goals.

Premiership Pals:

Robin van Persie (Man Utd) is the captain. Maarten Stekelenburg (Fulham), Tim Krul (Newcastle) and Michel Vorm (Swansea) should be the keepers. Then there's Ron Vlaar (Aston Villa), Erik Pieters (Stoke), John Heitinga (Everton/Fulham), Jonathan de Guzman (Swansea) and Leroy Fer (Norwich). In addition, Arjen Robben (ex-Chelsea), Rafael van der Vaart (ex-Spurs) and Dirk Kuyt (ex-Liverpool) have all done their time in our top league.

World Cup Previous:

The nearly-men of the World Cup, three times the bridesmaids but never the brides. They lit up the 1974 tournament, but stumbled at the last against the West Germans. Then they were runners up again in 1978, again succumbing to the hosts, this time Argentina. Last time out they failed in their uncharacteristic attempt to brutalise the Spanish in the final, with Heitinga sent off and de Jong lucky not to be.

CHILE

FIFA RANKING: 15   World cup wins: 0
Kit: Red shirts, blue shorts, white shorts.

World cup odds: 50-1 (13th favourites)

IT IS DIFFICULT TO TELL WHETHER HAVING THE WORLD CUP on their home continent is going to be much of an advantage for Chile. They won't have as far to travel as some, that's for sure, but while Chile extends northwards to a point closer to the equator than many of the venues, it also stretches longly and thinly down to the Southern tip of the continent, making them the most Southerly country ever to qualify. And where Brazil has millions of acres of humid Amazonian rainforest, Chile has the driest desert in the world, the Atacama, where it once didn't rain for forty years. So it could cut either way for them...

How they got there:

Chile finished third in the South American qualifying competition behind Argentina and Colombia despite a couple of heavy defeats. They showed that they can score goals, though, bagging 29, with Arturo Vidal their top scorer grabbing five.

How will they do?

They will have their work cut out in this difficult group, but they showed when they beat Roy Hodgson's experimental team 2-0 in November that they are no pushovers. They held the ball well, and England struggled to deal with the pace and mobility of their La Liga-based attackers, Vargas and Sánchez. At their best they are certainly capable of upsetting either the Spanish or the Dutch, or even both...?

The Manager:

Argentine Jorge Sampaoli took the top job in December 2012 after a successful stint in charge of the gloriously named club side Deportivo O'Higgins. He's a disciple of his countryman Marcelo Bielsa, and has introduced an energetic high-pressing style that has brought impressive results.

Watch out for:

Alexis Sánchez of Barcelona is lightning quick and can play anywhere in attack, and as well as the winning goal in this season's first El Clasico, he also notched twice as Chile beat England in last November's friendly at Wembley. Has been in outstanding goalscoring form in La Liga since moving from Serie A side Udinese three seasons ago.

Premiership Pals:

Jean Beausejour has twice been relegated from the Premiership, with Birmingham and Wigan, as well as being suspended from the national team for being drunk. Defender Gary Medel (named after Gary Lineker) has become a favourite at Cardiff, and Gonzalo Jara of Nottingham Forest could be heading for the top flight one way or another. Veteran David Pizarro played a handful of games for Manchester City.

World Cup Previous:

Chile hosted the World Cup in 1962 and finished in third place, losing 4-2 to Brazil in the semi-final and beating Yugoslavia in the third/ fourth playoff. After that, despite qualifying five times, they didn't even win another finals match until 2010. Talk about 48 years of hurt. In South Africa Chile made it into the last sixteen, where they came unstuck against Brazil.

AUSTRALIA

FIFA RANKING: 56   World cup wins: 0

Kit: Gold shirts, green shorts, gold socks.

World cup odds: 750-1 (=27th favourites)

AUS

OR MANY YEARS – DECADES, EVEN – AUSTRALIA'S WORLD Cup story was one of frustrating near misses. They were the giants of the Oceania Football Confederation, laying waste to the hapless minnows that dared to cross their mighty path, such as American Samoa who were gubbed 31-0 in 2001. However, there was never a direct route to the World Cup finals from Oceania, and they lost play offs variously to North Korea, Israel, Scotland, Iran, Argentina and Uruguay before deciding that enough was enough and applying to join the Asian Football Confederation instead. They seem likely to be habitual qualifiers from now on, with loads of air miles to boot.

How they got there:

Australia coasted past Oman, Thailand and Saudi Arabia in the AFC Third Round Group D, which meant they qualified for Fourth Round Group B, in which they finished in second place behind Japan. The crucial result was a 4-0 win over Jordan in the penultimate game, which funnily enough condemned their opponents to a tricky play-off with Uruguay.

How will they do?

It is difficult to see the Socceroos adding to their two World Cup finals victories, but they have enough about them to be awkward opponents for their more fancied rivals in the Group.

The Manager:

Ange Postecoglou took over after Holger Osieck paid the price for consecutive 0-6 defeats against France and Brazil. He is the most successful coach in Australian club football (with South Melbourne and Brisbane Roar), and played four times for the Socceroos in the 1980s.

Watch out for:

Josh Kennedy (Nagoya Grampus) glories in the nickname "Jesus", because of the long straggly hair and beard he used to sport. He is only going to be inspired by the massive statue of himself that gazes serenely down over Rio de Janeiro. As a striker he averages a goal every other game in Japanese football and for the Socceroos, and he scored the all-important goal that finally clinched qualification for Australia against Iraq.

Premiership Pals:

Mile Jedinak has been an important part of the Crystal Palace side. Tim Cahill (New York Red Bulls) had eight mightily effective years at Everton, while Lucas Neill turned out for Blackburn and West Ham. Mark Schwarzer (Chelsea) announced his international retirement before Christmas, but in a metatarsal emergency, maybe...?

World Cup Previous:

Australia qualified for the 1974 tournament, where their best result was a goalless draw against their first opponents this time, Chile. The Socceroos subsequently became known for their near misses until they finally qualified again in 2006. This was a so-called Golden Generation for Australia, and with Guus Hiddink in charge they went through to the knockout phase where they unluckily lost out to a late Italian penalty. In 2010 they qualified again, but missed out on progressing beyond the group stage on goal difference to Ghana.

GROUP

C

COLOMBIA

GREECE

IVORY COAST

JAPAN

GROUP C

14 JUNE	17:00 BBC	BELO HORIZONTE
COLOMBIA		GREECE

15 JUNE	02:00 ITV	RECIFE
IVORY COAST		JAPAN

19 JUNE	17:00 BBC	BRASILIA
COLOMBIA		IVORY COAST

19 JUNE	23:00 BBC	NATAL
JAPAN		GREECE

24 JUNE	21:00 BBC	CUIABA
JAPAN		COLOMBIA

24 JUNE	21:00 BBC	FORTALEZA
GREECE		IVORY COAST

	W	D	L	F	A	Pts

COLOMBIA

FIFA RANKING: 4   World cup wins: 0
Kit: Yellow shirts, whte shorts, white socks.
World cup odds: 25-1 (=7th favourites)

COL

Colombian football's golden period was the 1990s. With top players such as Carlos "Hair Bear" Valderrama, Freddy "Freddy" Rincon, Rene "El Loco" Higuita and Faustino "Keegan's Wet Dream" Asprilla they began shaking off the tag of South American also-rans. In the qualifying tournament for USA 94 they swept all before them, memorably thrashing Argentina 5-0 in Buenos Aires. Expectations were high, too high for poor Andres Escobar, who was assassinated after his own goal brought a shock early exit. They topped off their golden decade with a Copa America win in 2001, but then returned to wallow in the shallows until now, when a new golden generation has raised Colombian hopes sky high once again.

How they got there:

Colombia qualified with a game to spare in the South American qualifying competition, in which they finished second behind Argentina. Radamel Falcao scored nine goals.

How will they do?

Colombia will be the favourites to top Group C, and their experience of South American conditions makes them a decent outside bet to go deep into the knockout stages. In November they came to Europe, beating Belgium and drawing with the Netherlands, which suggests they should be able to hold their own against most opponents.

The Manager:

José Pékerman coached Argentina to the 2006 World Cup, and took over the Colombia team in 2012. He is so into it that he has become a naturalised Colombian. Pékerman's reputation is that he's a tinkerman, prone to inexplicably changing a winning team or try a new formation in a big game.

Watch out for:

A couple of weeks after Theo Walcott suffered the cruciate ligament injury that ruled him out of the World Cup, the same thing happened to AS Monaco's Colombian superstar Radamel Falcao. Unlike Theo, however, Falcao is hoping to recover in time to feature, and Colombian fans the world over have their fingers crossed. A social media movement entitled Fuerza Tigre (strong tiger) sprang up in his support, and the slogan has popped up everywhere. If Falcao doesn't make it Jackson Martinez, the F.C. Porto goal machine, might just make a name for himself in his place.

Premiership Pals:

Hugo Rodallega, formerly of Wigan and now of Fulham, has long been the only Colombian in the Premiership, but he hasn't figured for the national team for quite a while. Left back Pablo Armero joined West Ham on loan from Napoli for the second half of the season.

World Cup Previous:

Not as much as you'd think. An undistinguished making-up-the-numbers appearance in Chile in 1962 was their only credit until the 1990s, when an all-star team under-achieved in three World Cups in a row. Roger Milla did for them in 1990, and they failed to get out of the group stage in 1994 and 1998. Would have qualified as hosts in 1986, but ran out of money and handed the gig over to Mexico.

GREECE

FIFA RANKING: 12 World cup wins: 0

Kit: White shirts, white shorts, white socks, all with blue trim.

World cup odds: 250-1 (25th favourites)

GRE

"DOING A GREECE" IS THE PHRASE THAT GIVES HOPE to all the unfancied teams at a big tournament. Greece were 150-1 outsiders when they went to the 2004 European Championships in Portugal. They beat the hosts in the opening game, and again in the final, having eliminated defending champions France along the way. The Greeks were named World Team of the Year for this, got mobbed on their return home, and got to change their nickname from Ethniki (the national team) to Piratikos (The Pirate Ship), which is much better.

How they got there:

Greece finished second behind Bosnia & Herzegovina in UEFA Group G, even though they only managed 12 goals in their ten games, scraping home and away 1-0 wins over puny Liechtenstein. Fortunately they found sufficient firepower to clinch a 4-2 aggregate win over Romania in the playoff, with Mitroglou grabbing three.

How will they do?

The current Greek team's approach, like that of their illustrious 2004 predecessors, is based on getting the defence right first. They only conceded four goals in qualifying, and three of those came in the decisive defeat to Bosnia & Herzegovina. Whether they can turn this solidity into points will depend on whether they can make anything happen at the other end.

The Manager:

Fernando Santos is a Portuguese coach who managed the top club sides in Portugal and Greece before taking over as Greek coach in 2010. Led them to the quarter finals of Euro 2012. May be a fan of Eric Cantona, having once asked fans of PAOK; "Should we keep fooling ourselves, mistaking sardines for lobsters?"

Watch out for:

Sokratis Papastathopoulos may not have the silkiest ball skills, but he has the most syllables in his name of any of the players likely to feature at Brazil 2014, and has established himself a star of the Bundesliga. He uses his first name on the back of his shirt so that fans can afford to buy the replikit from the Borussia Dortmund club shop.

Premiership Pals:

Giorgos Karagounis of Fulham is the captain, with over 130 caps. Kostas Mitroglou joined him at the Cottage in the January transfer window for £12 million. Celtic's Georgios Samaras had a couple of seasons with Manchester City.

World Cup Previous:

Unlike their record in the European Championships, Greece's World Cup story has no real highlights. They have made it to the finals only twice before. In 1994 they lost all their games without scoring a goal, with the most memorable moment probably being Diego Maradona's terrifying spittle-spurting goal celebration a couple of inches from the touchline camera. And in 2010 they scored their only World Cup finals goals in coming from behind to take their only World Cup finals win against Nigeria in Bloemfontein.

IVORY COAST

FIFA RANKING: 17 World cup wins: 0
Kit: All orange.

World cup odds: 150-1 (=18th favourites)

CIV

IVORY COAST HAVE BEEN REGARDED AS A POWER IN African football for some time now, but in fact their achievements are relatively limited – two modest World Cup adventures, and three African Nations Cup finals, all of which were resolved by penalty shoot outs. It seems their reputation has been significantly enhanced by the high profile of one man, Didier Drogba, and anyone who thinks sport and politics don't mix should look away now. Drogba is credited with having brought about a cease fire in a five-year-long civil war, and he used the £3 million fee he got for endorsing Pepsi to build a hospital in his home town Abidjan.

How they got there:

Ivory Coast powered through African Group C, seeing off Morocco, Tanzania and Gambia with relative ease. They then came through a two-legged playoff against Senegal, winning 3-1 in Abidjan and surviving a second leg onslaught to draw 1-1 in neutral Casablanca.

How will they do?

Yaya Toure would walk into pretty much any team in the world, and though this might be Drogba's last hurrah he will want to go out with a bang not a whimper. Should have enough to progress from this group, and then who knows...?

The Manager:

Sabri Lamouchi is a former French international, who just missed the cut for France's triumphant 1998 World Cup squad. As a coach, however, he is something of an unknown quantity, only 42, and with no club management experience before taking over Les Éléphants in 2012.

Watch out for:

With Didier Drogba nearing the end, Ivory Coast are looking for a front man to share the burden and ultimately inherit the mantle of the great man. Wilfried Bony, who has made a fine impression in his first season with Swansea City, could be the fellow to step up. He's strong, he's mobile, he's good in the air, and his finishing is first-class. Also, he puts his first name on the back of his shirt, as if he hopes to be known only by that single title, and they do like that sort of thing in Brazil.

Premiership Pals:

Yaya Touré of Man City and Kolo Touré of Liverpool, Cheick Tioté (Newcastle), Arouna Koné (Everton), Wilfried Bony (Swansea), Yannick Sagbo (Hull City), and Abdul Razak (West Ham). Lacina Traoré joined Everton on loan from AS Monaco in January. There is also, of course, Didier Drogba, his ex-Chelsea team mate Salomon Kalou, and former-Gunner Gervinho to spot.

World Cup Previous:

Ivory Coast have qualified for the last two tournaments, each time finding themselves in a really tough group. In 2006 they lost to Argentina and the Netherlands, both by 2-1, before coming from two down to beat Serbia and Montenegro. Then in South Africa they drew with Portugal and lost to Brazil, a 3-0 win over North Korea not enough to take them any further.

JAPAN

FIFA RANKING: 48 World cup wins: 0
Kit: All dark blue.

World cup odds: 150-1 (=18th favourites)

JPN

D ESPITE THE TRAILBLAZING EFFORTS OF GARY LINEKER at Nagoya Grampus 8 in the early nineties, there have never been particularly strong links between Japanese football and ours. Japanese football fans look towards Brazil for their couch potato kicks, and their great heroes include the likes of Zico, who played for Kashima Antlers and managed the Japanese team for four years. Captain Tsubasa, a Manga comic character who is a sort of Japanese Roy of the Rovers, leaves his home country to make his name for São Paolo, the very apex of Japanese footballing ambition. Further adventures take him to Barcelona and the Bundesliga, but not to the Premier League – not yet, anyway.

How they got there:

Japan were the first team to qualify for the finals, but things didn't start altogether smoothly for them as they finished second in AFC Third Round Group C behind Uzbekistan. The next phase was rather more straightforward, and they topped their Fourth Round group ahead of Australia to qualify directly.

How will they do?

Japan didn't win a game in last year's Confederations Cup but they put in creditable performances, especially in a 3-4 loss to Italy, who they could meet again in the last 16. Brazilian football is very popular in Japan, so the venues and atmosphere will not be alien to them.

The Manager:

Alberto Zaccheroni is a 61-year-old Italian coach, veteran of several top Serie A jobs. He made his name with Udinese, won a scudetto with AC Milan, and enjoyed stints at Lazio, Inter, Torino and Juventus before landing the Japan job in 2010.

Watch out for:

Keisuke Honda joined AC Milan from CSKA Moscow in the January transfer window. He is an attacking midfielder, sometimes deployed as a 'false nine', known for his surging dribbling runs and his expertise with the dead ball. He won two Man of the Match awards at the 2010 World Cup, the judges perhaps swayed by his perfect execution of a Cruyff Turn (see p.182) against Denmark.

Premiership Pals:

Shinji Kagawa of Manchester United is the highest profile Japanese star in the Premiership, although David Moyes doesn't seem as impressed with him as he might be. Maya Yoshida plays centre back for Southampton. Tadanari Lee, who had a few games at St Mary's, has a couple of caps, as does Ryo Miyaichi of Arsenal (reserves).

World Cup Previous:

Japan have taken part in the last four tournaments, qualifying three times and co-hosting with South Korea in 2002. Their best performance was on home soil, when fanatical support lifted them to wins over Russia and Tunisia and a draw with Belgium. They reached the knockout stage, where they succumbed to Turkey. Then in 2010 they matched that run, beating Cameroon and Denmark before going out on penalties to Paraguay in the last 16.

GROUP

D

ENGLAND

ITALY

COSTA RICA

URUGUAY

GROUP D

14 JUNE	20:00 ITV		FORTALEZA
URUGUAY			COSTA RICA

14 JUNE	23:00 BBC		MANAUS
ENGLAND			ITALY

19 JUNE	20:00 ITV		SAO PAULO
URUGUAY			ENGLAND

20 JUNE	17:00 BBC		RECIFE
ITALY			COSTA RICA

24 JUNE	17:00 ITV		NATAL
ITALY			URUGUAY

24 JUNE	17:00 ITV		BELO HORIZONTE
COSTA RICA			ENGLAND

	W	D	L	F	A	Pts

COSTA RICA

FIFA RANKING: 31   World cup wins: 0

Kit: Red shirts with a white stripe, blue shorts with a white stripe, white socks (possibly with a white stripe, it's hard to tell).

World cup odds: 2000-1 (31st favourites)

CRC

OSTA RICA IS JUST TO THE NORTH OF PANAMA, WITH a Pacific coast to the West, and a Caribbean coastline to the East. It is known for its progressive environmental policies, and has the reputation as one of the greenest countries in the world. A quarter of its area is given over to national parks or refuges, and ten percent of the world's butterflies can be found there. It is a Spanish-speaking nation, with some nice sayings. Your partner is referred to as your *media naranja*, or the other half of your orange. And if you ask someone how they are doing they are likely to reply "*Pura vida!*" which means "pure life!"

How they got there:

The Ticos won all of their home matches, ending second in the CON-CACAF qualifying competition behind the USA. Ominously, however, they didn't win any away games, appealing against a defeat in Denver on the grounds that the weather was a bit unpleasant.

How will they do?

Costa Rica are long-odds outsiders for the tournament, and not expected to progress through a difficult group. However, when the draw was made it put a smile on the face of Jurgen Klinsmann, who warned the English media not to under-rate their Central American opponents, as he had before his USA team were well beaten in the return leg following the Denver blizzard. They can play a bit, apparently.

The Manager:

Jorge Luis Pinto is a much-travelled 61-year-old Colombian coach, who failed to take his home country to the last World Cup, but has fared much better this time around with Costa Rica.

Watch out for:

Álvaro Saborío scored eight goals in qualifying, and is a prolific marksman for Real Salt Lake in Major League Soccer. He is a somewhat volatile character, having a track record of missing penalties he has insisted upon taking against his coach's better judgement, and once got into trouble for booting the ball at a kid who was taunting him.

Premiership Pals:

Bryan Oviedo (Everton) and Bryan Ruiz (Fulham) are conspiring to bring the name Bryan (not seen since the retirement of a former England captain) back into common usage in the top flight. Unfortunately this cunning plan has been thwarted by Oviedo's nasty double leg break (which means he won't feature) and Ruiz's loan to PSV Eindhoven.

World Cup Previous:

Costa Rica have qualified for three World Cup tournaments. In 1990 they beat Scotland and Sweden on their way to the knockout phase, where they got well-beaten by Czechoslovakia. In 2002 they played some extremely vibrant stuff led by Paolo Wanchope and were only knocked out on goal difference. In Germany four years later they had a bit of a nightmare, losing all their games despite being fancied to progress.

ENG

ENGLAND

FIFA RANKING: 13 World cup wins: 1
(and two world wars)

Kit: White shirts, dark blue shorts, white socks, three lions (on shirt).

World cup odds: 33-1 (=11th favourites)

I F NOTHING ELSE, IT WOULD AT LEAST MAKE A CHANGE IF England could win a penalty shootout in Brazil. Since drawn knockout games have been decided by the Elfmeterschiessen method no international team has such a poor record as we have, winning just one out of seven. And even on that one occasion we lost another one the very next time out. To the Germans, naturally. So let's hope that this time a list featuring otherwise illustrious names such as Pearce, Waddle, Southgate, Batty, Ince, Beckham, Vassell, Lampard, Gerrard, Carragher, Young and Cole (A) gets no longer. There simply aren't enough Pizza Hut adverts to go round...

How they got there:

England finished on top of UEFA Group H by a point from Ukraine, after a slightly uninspiring campaign in which they drew games they should have won, but then won games they had to win..

How will they do?

Time will tell whether Greg Dyke's pessimistic throat-cutting mime was the correct response to being dumped in the Group of Geoff, but Roy's boys could certainly take something from games with Uruguay and Italy, and it may all come down to who does best against Costa Rica. England play them last, which might just be the handiest thing about a difficult draw.

The Manager:

Roy Hodgson took Switzerland to the World Cup in 1994, where he and Jack Charlton were England's only representatives. An impressive tactician, and maybe more likely to take a chance than either Eriksson or Capello.

Watch out for:

We know all about Wayne Rooney and Steven Gerrard, but it would be nice, wouldn't it, if one of the up-and-coming young stars stepped up and made a name for themselves? Two have already shown that they are undaunted by playing in or against Brazil. Jack Wilshere's performance when England beat Brazil at Wembley in February 2013 seemed at the time like the most significant breakthrough since Gazza's. And Alex Oxlade-Chamberlain's stunningly confident strike in the Maracanã last June hinted that he might have what it takes to have a top campaign.

Premiership Pals:

All of England's likely squad play in the Premiership, possibly because they lack the nerve, the ambition and the mental fortitude to try and make it abroad. The only exceptions are goalkeeper Fraser Forster, who plays for Celtic, and Jermaine Defoe who just moved to Toronto, but neither of them are nailed-on certainties to go.

World Cup Previous:

One win, back in the days when it was all right to play World Cup matches at places like Ayresome Park or Goodison without pulling them down and replacing them with fabulously expensive white elephants, and one captivating run to semi-final penalty shootout heartbreak to the strains of Nessun Dorma. Apart from that no fewer than six campaigns have ended at the quarter final stage.

ITALY

FIFA RANKING: 7 World cup wins: 4
Kit: Blue shirts, whte shorts, blue socks.
World cup odds: 25-1 (=7th favourites)

ITA

HISTORICALLY THE *AZZURRI* HAVE ALWAYS BEEN contenders, but in recent years expectations of their fanatical supporters may have lessened slightly following their worst-ever showing in South Africa. They were fêted for their performance in reaching the final of Euro 2012, even though they were thrashed 4-0 by Spain, and pleased also with their third place in the Confederations Cup, as though accepting that they were never going to beat Brazil. They approach tournaments with caution and apprehension, burdened with a fear of failure even greater than England's. So it might be a good thing to be playing them first.

How they got there:

Italy topped UEFA Group B, six points clear of Denmark, with the same six-wins-four-draws record as England. It was an uninspiring, pragmatic campaign in which Italy did just enough, not bothering to put the likes of Malta to the sword.

How will they do?

After Italy knocked England out of Euro 2012 the UK media were drooling over their technical superiority and possession stats, but, smart as some of Andrea Pirlo's passing was, they still didn't score a goal in 120 minutes. If anything they have a tendency to settle – settle for a draw or a narrow win, rather than killing teams off – which leaves them vulnerable to late comebacks.

The Manager:

Cesare Prandelli took over after the last World Cup, having made his name at Fiorentina without ever challenging for a *scudetto*. His international results have been OK, but his team has tended to enjoy possession without being prepared to take risks. And he has a 0-1 defeat to the Faroe Islands on his CV.

Watch out for:

Mario Balotelli is one of the most eye-catching players in world football, equally likely to light up a game with a piece of brilliance or to set fire to the team hotel by letting fireworks off in the bathroom. He showed, with his destruction of Germany in the semi-final of Euro 2012, that he can turn a match single-handedly, but if things aren't going his way he is prone to lashing out and walking the walk.

Premiership Pals:

Italy continue to select their squads almost exclusively from Serie A, but Emanuele Giaccherini of Sunderland has kept his place despite leaving Juventus, while Dani Osvaldo has been sent to Juventus on loan from Southampton after a fight. Alberto Aquilani didn't really fit in at Liverpool. Giusepppe Rossi was a kid at Old Trafford. And we all remember Mario Balotelli, don't we?

World Cup Previous:

Italy have won the trophy four times, in 1934, 1938, 1982 and 2006, and have been runners up twice, both times to Brazil, in 1970 and 1994 (Baggio... oh no!). 1982 is best remembered for the goals of Rossi and the celebration of Tardelli, while 2006 will always be the final where Zidane head-butted Materazzi in the chest. Every now and then – 1986, 2002, 2010 – Italy mess things up, go home early, and get pelted with fruit by their own supporters at the airport.

URUGUAY

FIFA RANKING: 6   World cup wins: 2
Kit: Pale blue shirts, black shorts, black socks.
World cup odds: 28-1 (= 9th)

URU

URUGUAY IS THE TOP-SEEDED TEAM IN GROUP D, EVEN though geographically they are minnows. The country is the second-smallest in South America, larger only than Suriname, with a population of only 3.3 million. Only five nations with a smaller talent pool have competed at a World Cup finals (Northern Ireland, Wales, Slovenia, Jamaica and Trinidad & Tobago), let alone won it (twice), so they really punch above their weight.

How they got there:

Given Uruguay's strong showing in South Africa and their high ranking, it was surprising that they seemed to struggle in qualifying. They only finished fifth in the South American qualifying process and were obliged to undergo a two-legged play off against Jordan, who they dispatched 5-0. Luis Suárez was the top scorer in South American qualifiers, though, notching 11 times.

How will they do?

Uruguay can be great going forward, but the defence might be a bit of a problem, thanks to a so-called 'golden generation' that is now starting to go over the hill together. Top teams may find a way through them with relative ease, but they will have to keep Cavani, Suárez and Forlán at bay. Likely to win and/or lose games 3-2, but could scramble through.

The Manager:

Óscar Tabárez is known as El Maestro, because he used to be a primary school teacher. His innovative use of the naughty step has proved ideal for dealing with modern professional footballers.

Watch out for:

Edinson Cavani's prolific scoring record in Serie A for Napoli aroused the interest of (naturally) Chelsea, Manchester City and Real Madrid, but he ended up moving to French moneybags outfit Paris St Germain last summer for 64.5 million Euros, where he has carried on in much the same rich vein of form. Likely to score while the opposition are looking for Suárez, who has been on fire this year, one of the most exciting players in the world. Even if he does look like a short-arsed Freddie Mercury.

Premiership Pals:

Luis Suárez (Liverpool), Sebastian Coates (Liverpool reserves), Diego Lugano (West Bromwich Albion), Gaston Ramirez (Southampton). Also there's Diego Forlán, the best player of the 2010 tournament, who used to ply his trade at Old Trafford but now plays in Japan.

World Cup Previous:

Uruguay certainly have World Cup previous. They hosted and won the first tournament in 1930, beating Argentina 4-2 in the final in Montevideo. Then, after missing the 1934 and 1938 shindigs, they won again in 1950 by beating hosts Brazil 2-1 in a packed Maracanã stadium. Since that momentously unpopular victory La Celeste's best finish has been fourth place, in 1954, 1970, and again last time, in 2010, thanks in part to a last-minute handball by Suárez in the quarter final against Ghana

GROUP

E

SWITZERLAND

ECUADOR

FRANCE

HONDURAS

GROUP E

15 JUNE	17:00 ITV	BRASILIA
SWITZERLAND		ECUADOR

15 JUNE	20:00 BBC	PORTO ALEGRE
FRANCE		HONDURAS

20 JUNE	20:00 ITV	SALVADOR
SWITZERLAND		FRANCE

20 JUNE	23:00 ITV	CURITIBA
HONDURAS		ECUADOR

25 JUNE	21:00 BBC	MANAUS
HONDURAS		SWITZERLAND

25 JUNE	21:00 BBC	RIO DE JANEIRO
ECUADOR		FRANCE

	W	D	L	F	A	Pts

SWITZERLAND'S WORLD CUP RECORD IS POOR, AND THEY have never really been much of a force in Europe, so their appearance in the first pot of seeds at last December's draw was something of a surprise, especially considering that Italy, France and, yes, England, were languishing amongst the also-rans. Their FIFA ranking is incredibly good, and this is down to two factors. Firstly they finished top of a really easy qualifying group, and secondly they have stopped playing friendlies against much more lowly-ranked teams, realising that even a win against a Liechtenstein or a Luxembourg (both regular opponents until recently), reduces your points average.

How they got there:

Switzerland sauntered through a soft UEFA Group E, finishing seven points clear of Iceland, with whom they drew 4-4. They spread the goals around, Fabian Schär top scoring with three, five others grabbing two...

How will they do?

They are the top seeds of this group, but France will be the favourites to win it, and Ecuador could be a handful for them too. They only notched seventeen in ten qualifiers against pretty mediocre opposition, and they don't really have a stand out striker. Bayer Leverkusen's Eren Derdiyok got a hat trick in a friendly against Germany, but apart from that his international goals have been few and far between.

The Manager:

Ottmar Hitzfeld is a veteran German whose playing and coaching career has alternated between Germany and Switzerland. Twice World Coach of the Year, having won the Champions League with both Borussia Dortmund and Bayern Munich.

Watch out for:

Xherdan Shaqiri (if only they allowed proper names in Scrabble..) is a naturalised Swiss whose family were refugees from the conflict in what was Yugoslavia. He's a stocky, muscular left-footed 22 year-old winger, who is part of the impressive squad being assembled by Bayern Munich. Last season he contributed to their treble, having done the double with FC Basel the season before.

Premiership Pals:

Former Gunner Phillippe Senderos was at Fulham until he left for Valencia in January. Still at the Cottage is Pajtim Kasami. Arsenal's Johan Djourou has been on a season-long loan at Hamburger SV. Valon Behrami played for West Ham, and Gelson Fernandes had two seasons at Man City.

World Cup Previous:

Three times quarter-finalists, in 1934, 1938 and 1954, but when Roy Hodgson took them to USA 94 it was their first World Cup appearance since 1966. In America they played in the first indoor World Cup game at the Pontiac Silverdome, and reached the last 16, where Spain were too good for them. In Germany they again reached the knockout phase, losing on penalties to Ukraine. Last time they went home early, despite being the only team to beat Spain.

ECUADOR

FIFA RANKING: 23   World cup wins: 0
Kit: Yellow shirt, blue shorts, red socks.
World cup odds: 140-1 (17th favourites)

ECU

THE HIGHEST MOUNTAIN PEAK ABOVE SEA LEVEL IS Mount Everest, everyone knows that. But the furthest point on the Earth's surface from the centre of the planet is the top of Mount Chimborazo in Ecuador, on account of the equatorial bulge. In the 19th century, Mount Chimborazo was thought to be the highest peak on Earth (above sea level), leading to numerous attempts to climb it. Quito, not far away, is the highest capital city in the world, and since Ecuador started playing regular qualification games there they have had a considerable advantage over teams that have not had time to acclimatise.

How they got there:

Ecuador secured fourth place in the South American qualification table ahead of Uruguay on goal difference. The crucial result was a victory over their nearest rivals in the penultimate game, but they also beat fellow qualifiers Chile and Colombia along the way. Felipe Caicedo of Al-Jazira contributed seven goals.

How will they do?

Ecuador might have liked a game or two at Manaus, although actually the home advantage they can usually call on is altitude rather than heat or humidity. They are not fancied to do well, but no team with seven Barcelona players in their ranks should be taken lightly (even if it is Barcelona Sporting Club, of Guayaquil in Ecuador).

The Manager:

Reinaldo Rueda is yet another jobbing Colombian coach at these finals. Previously coached his home country, then took Honduras to South Africa, before taking over Ecuador.

Watch out for:

Antonio Valencia first caught the eye as a flying winger for Wigan Athletic, and he landed a big money move to Manchester United in the summer of 2009. Alex Ferguson clearly hoped that he would be the new Cristiano Ronaldo, and he has certainly eclipsed Nani, the previous new Cristiano Ronaldo, in his time at Old Trafford. He had a lean time in 2012-13, though, which he superstitiously blamed on his having taken over the number 7 shirt, and he couldn't wait to get his old number 25 - and with it his mojo - back. Unfortunately for Antonio, World Cup squads only go up to 23. I am also going to be looking out for Elvis Bone, one of the great footballer names, if he makes the squad.

Premiership Pals:

Antonio Valencia, the captain, (Manchester United, and before that Wigan Athletic) is the lone Ecuadorean in the Premiership, although Segundo Castillo played a few times on loan at Everton and Wolves, and Felipe Caicedo was at Manchester City for a while.

World Cup Previous:

Ecuador have qualified twice before, in 2002 and 2006. The highlight of the first of these was a 1-0 over Croatia, who had finished third in the previous tournament. In 2006 they beat Poland and Costa Rica to follow group winners Germany into the last 16, where they were eliminated by a David Beckham free kick.

FRANCE

FIFA RANKING: 19   World cup wins: 1
Kit: Dark blue shirts, white shorts, red socks.
World cup odds: 22-1 (6th favourites)

FRA

MICHEL PLATINI IS THE HANNIBAL SMITH OF international football – he loves it when a plan comes together. At the draw back in December, *Les Bleus* were staring down the barrel. One surplus European team would have to move into a pot with the African and South American teams, thus facing a top seed and also another European giant. Every other time this situation has arisen it has been the team with the lowest ranking that has been moved, i.e. France. But Platini suddenly introduced another extra little draw, thus contriving that Italy were dumped into the monster Group of Geoff with England and Uruguay, while France landed in the Group of Marshmallow, with Toytown, a Girl Guides XI and the Oompa-Loompas.

How they got there:

France were second in UEFA Group I, three points behind Spain. This meant a playoff against Ukraine, and the game looked all up after they lost the first leg 0-2 in Kiev, with Laurent Koscielny sent off. However they turned things round dramatically with a 3-0 second leg win, courtesy of Sakho (2) and Benzema.

How will they do?

It looks plain sailing for the lucky French boys, thanks to Platini's efforts. However, Argentina and Germany are in their half later on, unless he can get them kicked out or forced to play with eight men.

The Manager:

Didier Deschamps won it all as a player, captaining France to the World Cup and the European Championship, and Marseille to the Champions League.

Watch out for:

Franck Ribéry joined Cristiano Ronaldo and Lionel Messi on the shortlist for the FIFA Ballon d'Or, and there were those who thought he should have won Blatter's bauble, as he was a member of the team that won the Champions League. He's a fast and tricky wide player, who is right-footed but prefers to play on the left so he can cut infield. Bayern Munich use him this way, but France don't always.

Premiership Pals:

Captain Hugo Lloris and Etienne Capoue (Spurs), Patrice Evra (Manchester Utd), Laurent Koscielny, Olivier Giroud and Bacary Sagna (Arsenal), Mamadou Sakho (Liverpool), Samir Nasri and Gael Clichy (Man City), Alou Diarra (West Ham), Loic Remy, Moussa Sissoko, Mathieu Debuchy, Mapou Yanga-Mbiwa (all Newcastle, as was Yohan Cabaye until recently). There's also Paul Pogba, the one who got away from Old Trafford.

World Cup Previous:

France, inspired by the genius of Zinedine Zidane, lifted the trophy on home soil in 1998. They reached the final again in 2006, but, let down by the headbutt of Zinedine Zidane, they lost out to the Italians. They reached the semi-finals in 1982 and 1986, losing out to West Germany on both occasions. The first of these was a brilliant 3-3 draw, marred by the horrific arse-first assault perpetrated by Harald Schumacher on Patrick Battiston, for which he wasn't even booked. He should have been incarcerated.

HONDURAS

FIFA RANKING: 42   *World cup wins:* 0

Kit: White shirts with pale blue pinstripes, white shorts, white socks.

World cup odds: 2500-1 (32nd favourites)

HON

HONDURAS MAY HAVE AN UNDISTINGUISHED WORLD Cup record, but they are the only finalists who have taken part in a World Cup war. Tensions between El Salvador and Honduras erupted into violence at the qualifying games for the 1970 World Cup, and ultimately developed into full-blown war between the two countries. The issue was that 300,000 Salvadoran peasants who had migrated over the border were living on land owned by wealthy Hondurans, who wanted it back. Instead of hiring seven mismatched mercenaries to fight their battles for them, as is standard practice, these peasants vented their dismay at the matches in Tegucigalpa and San Salvador.

How they got there:

Honduras finished third in the CONCAF qualification table behind USA and Costa Rica, beating both along the way, and obliging perennial qualifiers Mexico (who they also beat) to play off for the honour. Jerry Bengtson and Carlo Costly grabbed four goals apiece.

How will they do?

Honduras are being written off pretty casually, considering they are up against the puniest of the top seeds and the lowest-ranked European and South American qualifiers. Honduras are no mugs, and beat all three of their fellow CONCACAF qualifiers to get to Brazil. Could easily snag a point or two.

The Manager:

Luis Suárez – no, not that one, this is Luis Fernando Suárez – is a Colombian, with much experience of South American football and conditions having also been manager of Ecuador. Indeed, he guided them to their best World Cup performance, in 2006.

Watch out for:

Carlo Costly is a favourite of the Honduran fans, averaging a goal every other game for the national side. Quite apart from his skills and his effort, though, he's going to catch the eye and ear because he sounds like a character in a Roy of the Rovers cartoon strip written by Ron Atkinson. One of the very few players whose replica shirt can be worn as a satirical comment on the nature of the modern game.

Premiership Pals:

Maynor Figueroa, formerly of Wigan and now of Hull City (or Hull Tigers if that nonsense has happened by the time you read this), has over 100 caps for Honduras. Wilson Palacios of Stoke City is nearing that same landmark. Roger Espinoza played in the Premiership and won an F.A. Cup winners medal for Wigan. His current team mate, Juan Carlos Garcia, arrived too late to do so.

World Cup Previous:

Honduras qualified for the 1982 World Cup in Spain, drawing 1-1 with the hosts and with group winners Northern Ireland, before defeat by Yugoslavia ended their adventure. They made it again last time, and a goalless draw in the third match against Switzerland eliminated both teams at the first hurdle. They meet again in the third group game this time, in what will be an unlikely grudge rematch.

GROUP

F

ARGENTINA   BOSNIA-HERZEGOVINA

IRAN   NIGERIA

GROUP F

15 JUNE	23:00 BBC	RIO DE JANEIRO
ARGENTINA		BOSNIA-HERZEGOVINA

16 JUNE	20:00 BBC	CURITIBA
IRAN		NIGERIA

21 JUNE	17:00 ITV	BELO HORIZONTE
ARGENTINA		IRAN

21 JUNE	23:00 BBC	CUIABA
NIGERIA		BOSNIA-HERZEGOVINA

25 JUNE	17:00 ITV	PORTO ALEGRE
NIGERIA		ARGENTINA

25 JUNE	17:00 ITV	SALVADOR
BOSNIA-HERZEGOVINA		IRAN

	W	D	L	F	A	Pts

ARGENTINA

ARG

FIFA RANKING: 3 World cup wins: 2
Kit: Pale blue and white striped shirt, white shorts, white socks, pale blue trim.
World cup odds: 9-2 (2nd favs)

ARGENTINA ARE AMONG THE BIG HITTERS OF WORLD football, and it really is a hotbed of the game. The *Superclasico* between River Plate and Boca Juniors is one of the world's great club game spectacles, and 90 per cent of the population claim to support a football team. Football was introduced to the country by British emigrants in Buenos Aires, most of whom were working on British-owned railway projects, and the league they established is the fourth oldest in the world, after the ones in England, Scotland and the Netherlands.

How they got there:

Convincing winners of the South American qualifying tournament, Argentina made it with something to spare. They only lost two games, and top scored with 35 goals, including 10 for Lionel Messi and 9 for Gonzalo Higuain.

How will they do?

With the likes of Messi, Higuain and Agüero to call upon, surely Argentina can't mess up the group stages. Then in the last sixteen they will meet a team from weedy-looking Group E, so the last eight looks absolutely nailed on, and it may be semi-final time before they are really tested.

The Manager:

Alejandro "Alex" Sabella was the smily curly-headed lad signed by Happy Harry Haslam to play for Sheffield United in 1978, as he was cheaper than the teenage Diego Maradona. He is an honorary Yorkshireman, in fact, as he also played for Leeds, and now looks uncannily like Brian Flynn.

Watch out for:

This World Cup is surely Lionel Messi's chance to topple Maradona from the highest perch in the Argentine soccer pantheon. If he can lead the Albiceleste to the trophy – in Brazil, of all places – then surely he can claim parity at least with the barrel-chested butterball. Probably the best player in the world, whatever Cristiano says.

Premiership Pals:

Sergio Kun Agüero (Man City), Fabricio Coloccini (Newcastle Utd), Jonás Gutiérrez (Newcastle Utd), Pablo Zabaleta (Man City). Erik Lamela of Spurs has probably not done enough this season, and Claudio Yacob of West Brom has been on the fringes of things. Former Liverpool stars Javier Mascherano and Maxi Rodríguez are still going, however.

World Cup Previous:

Argentina have won the World Cup twice. As the hosts in 1978 they swept to the title in gorgeous hailstorms of confetti courtesy of the goals of Mario Kempes and the pots of (alleged) bribe money of the governing generals, which supposedly persuaded Peru to roll over 6-0 in the decisive semi-final group game. In 1986 the unstoppable brilliance and basketball skills of Diego Maradona brought them the trophy once again. They have also been runners up twice, in 1930 and 1990. Last time they played some brilliant stuff before being caned 4-0 by the Germans in the quarters.

BOSNIA-HERZEGOVINA

BIH

FIFA RANKING: 19 World cup wins: 0
Kit: Blue shirts, blue shorts, blue socks.
World cup odds: 175-1 (=23rd favourites)

Bosnia & Herzegovina are the latest of the constituent parts of the former Yugoslavia to make it to a World Cup, following Croatia (1998, 2002, 2006, 2014), Serbia & Montenegro (2006), Serbia (2010) and Slovenia (2002, 2010). The capital city, Sarajevo, was besieged for nearly four years during the Bosnian War for Independence (1992-96), and was also the place where Archduke Franz Ferdinand of Austria was assassinated in 1914, precipitating the start of World War I. All of which rather overshadows the fact that it was also where Torvill and Dean won Winter Olympic gold in 1984.

How they got there:

Bosnia & Herzegovina topped UEFA Group G ahead of Greece on goal difference. As well as beating their nearest rivals 3-1 in the decisive game, they also scored a load more goals, with Edin Džeko bagging ten and Vedad Ibišević eight.

How will they do?

They have some decent players, many of whom play in Germany or in Turkey, and certainly seem capable of scoring goals against anybody. Could make it through to the last 16 at the first time of asking.

The Manager:

Safet Sušić was an attacking midfielder for FK Sarajevo, Paris St Germain and Yugoslavia in the seventies and eighties, and France Football voted him the best ever foreign player to grace Ligue 1.

Watch out for:

Zvjezdan Misimović has somehow managed to win more caps for Bosnia & Herzegovina than any other player, despite a turbulent relationship with the national set-up. He once led a player revolt, refusing to play until certain members of the Bosnian F.A. resigned. After this he became captain, but when a new coach stripped him of the armband he retired at 25. A new coach talked him into returning and made him captain again, before accusing Misimović of faking injury to undermine him and dropping him. Misimović retired again until that coach left, coming back under Sušić to play an important part in qualifying.

Premiership Pals:

There are two high-profile Premiership players from Bosnia & Herzegovina - Asmir Begović, Stoke City's much-coveted goalkeeper, and Edin Džeko, arguably the most likely of all Manchester City's elite strikers to boot the ball into the top tier from six yards out.

World Cup Previous:

Bosnia & Herzegovina are the only team making their World Cup finals debut in Brazil. Formerly they were part of Yugoslavia, who, with Bosnian coach Safet Sušić in the team, reached the quarter finals of Italia 90. They first tried to qualify in their own right for the 1998 World Cup, and have gradually been getting closer and closer, narrowly missing out on the 2010 tournament in a playoff with Portugal, until finally now they have hit the jackpot.

IRAN

FIFA RANKING: 34   World cup wins: 0

Kit: White shirts with red and green trim, white shorts, white socks.

IRN

World cup odds: 1500-1 (30th favourites)

I RAN'S ADVENTURES AT THE 1998 WORLD CUP IN FRANCE were the subject of a television documentary called The Outsiders, made by British comedians Andy Smart and Nick Hancock (whose wife is Iranian). The Iranian players, including all-time great Ali Daei, came across as charming, civilised fellows – especially compared to the bunch we had at the time, which had Gazza in it – and the film was touching, and funny, and really made you root for them, especially against the Americans...

How they got there:

Iran have had to get through more rounds of qualifying than the other three Asian qualifiers, beginning with a two-leg defeat of the Maldives. Then they topped a third round group, thus qualifying for the last stage. This was another group, which Iran again topped, ahead of fellow qualifiers South Korea, Uzbekistan, Qatar and Lebanon. Javad Nekounam scored six qualifying goals.

How will they do?

Iran will not be fancied, but they could have ended up in a much tougher group than this one. A point or two is far from out of the question, and on a good day, who knows...?

The Manager:

Carlos Queiroz will be familiar as the guy who replaced Steve McClaren as Fergie's assistant, either side of a brief interlude as coach of Real Madrid. Has also twice been boss of his native Portugal, and the South African national team.

Watch out for:

Carlos Queiroz has been canny, scouring the world game for players with links to the Iranian diaspora and bringing them into the squad. Daniel Davari is a German-born goalkeeper from Eintracht Braunshweig, Steve Beitashour is a Californian MLS All-Star, and Reza Ghoochannejhad grew up and learnt his football in the Netherlands. Probably his biggest coup, though, is recruiting rapid winger Ashkan Dejagah to his ranks. Dejagah was a key member of the Vfl Wolfsburg team that won the Bundesliga back in 2009, and he played for Germany in all the age groups below senior level before opting to switch to Iran.

Premiership Pals:

Ashkan Dejagah flourished in the Bundesliga before joining Fulham in 2012. In January Reza Ghochannejhad joined Charlton Athletic, who are not currently looking likely to return to the Premiership, but they do have previous links with Iran, having got fifteen minutes of Premiership action out of Iran legend Karim Bagheri once upon a time.

World Cup Previous:

Iran first qualified in 1978, where they embarrassed Scotland by holding them to a 1-1 draw, even scoring their goal for them. The Iran-Iraq war put paid to football for the 1980s, but they returned to finals action in 1998. In France they scored a notable victory in a sensitive fixture against the USA. Then in 2006 they managed a single point from a 1-1 draw with Angola

NIGERIA

FIFA RANKING: 41   World cup wins: 0
Kit: All green.

World cup odds: 200-1 (24th favourites)

NGA

NIGERIA IS KNOWN AS "THE GIANT OF AFRICA". ITS population of over 174 million makes it the most heavily-populated country in the continent, and seventh in the world. Oil has brought great revenues to the country, making Nigeria's economy the second-largest in Africa, and it is expected to surpass South Africa in the very near future. Its capital city since 1991, Abuja, is a modern planned city, much like Brasilia, with which it is twinned. Nigeria achieved independence from the United Kingdom in 1960, and remains a member of the Commonwealth.

How they got there:

After an unbeaten qualifying campaign in which Nigeria conceded only four goals, they clinched their place in Brazil by beating Ethiopia in the playoff. Emmanuel Emenike scored both goals in a 2-1 away win, and Victor Moses and Victor Obinna notched in the 2-0 second leg victory.

How will they do?

The current African champions, though if they fulfil Pele's prediction that an African team will win the World Cup in his own back yard the old boy will probably collapse with shock. Nigeria seem seriously under-rated, and must have a chance of emulating their best run to the last 16.

The Manager:

Stephen Keshi is one of only two people to have won the African Nations Cup as a player and as a coach. He also coached Togo, guiding them to qualification for the 2006 World Cup before being replaced by Otto Pfister, then getting the job back again afterwards.

Watch out for:

Vincent Enyeama, the Lille goalkeeper, was just a 19-year-old kid when he kept a clean sheet against England in Osaka in 2002. He made some blinding saves that day from Owen and Sheringham. Now, nearly 100 caps later, he is the rock at the back for the Super Eagles, having been named as the top keeper at the most recent African Nations Cup, and he's the captain as well.

Premiership Pals:

Shola Ameobi (Newcastle), John Obi Mikel (Chelsea), Victor Moses (Liverpool). Peter Odemwingie (Stoke City) has currently fallen out with Stephen Keshi. Sone Aluko of Hull City has a couple of Nigeria caps to his name, even though his sister Eniola plays for England. Then there's Obafemi Martins (now Seattle Sounders, once Newcastle, Birmingham City), and Victor Obinna (now Chievo, once played for West Ham).

World Cup Previous:

Nigeria first qualified in 1994, topping their group ahead of Argentina, and coming within two minutes of knocking out Italy before Baggio came to the rescue. They made it to the last 16 again in 1998, where they were knocked out by Denmark. In 2002 they finished bottom of England's group, picking up just one point. A similar disappointing return from the group stage in 2010 saw the team withdrawn from international competition by Nigerian President Goodluck Jonathan.

GROUP

G

GERMANY

PORTUGAL

GHANA

UNITED STATES

GROUP G

16 JUNE		17:00 ITV		SALVADOR
GERMANY			**PORTUGAL**	

16 JUNE		23:00 BBC		NATAL
GHANA			**UNITED STATES**	

21 JUNE		20:00 BBC		FORTALEZA
GERMANY			**GHANA**	

22 JUNE		23:00 BBC		MANAUS
UNITED STATES			**PORTUGAL**	

26 JUNE		17:00 BBC		RECIFE
UNITED STATES			**GERMANY**	

26 JUNE		17:00 BBC		BRASILIA
PORTUGAL			**GHANA**	

	W	D	L	F	A	Pts

GERMANY

FIFA RANKING: 2   World cup wins: 3
Kit: All white, with red chevron on chest.
World cup odds: 11-2 (3rd favourites)

GER

G ERMANY (OR WEST GERMANY) HAVE COMPETED IN every World Cup finals tournament bar two. They didn't enter in 1930, and they missed out in 1950, the last time the finals were held in Brazil. At the time the country was still occupied and partitioned after the Second World War, and neither they nor Japan were permitted to compete. Curiously, however, FIFA had recognised Saarland, part of Germany that was then occupied by France, but not in time for them to try and qualify. Saarland did enter in 1954, and, managed by Helmut Schoen (later a World Cup-winning manager) finished just behind West Germany in their qualifying group.

How they got there:

Germany won all their matches in UEFA Group C bar one, an astonishing game in Berlin in which they led Sweden 4-0 after an hour, but ended up with a 4-4 draw. They scored freely in qualifying (especially against Ireland), Mesut Özil their top scorer with eight.

How will they do?

The Germans may be England's bogey team (1966 notwithstanding), but they will be hoping not to come up against the Italians, having never beaten them in a major tournament game. They could meet in the semi-finals again this time...

The Manager:

Joachim "Jogi" Löw was Jurgen Klinsmann's assistant at the 2006 World Cup, and he was known to be the tactical strategist of the two. They introduced a vibrant attacking philosophy which Löw has continued in his eight years as the number one, and he is also credited with bringing on a generation of younger German stars.

Watch out for:

Thomas Müller was awarded the Golden Boot at the 2010 World Cup, despite being tied on five goals with David Villa, Wesley Schneider and Diego Forlán, after FIFA suddenly decided to introduce assists and minutes played as extra criteria. The muscular young Bayern Munich attacker showed admirable pace and technique four years ago, not least in the humbling of Capello's England in Bloemfontein, and has continued to develop into a considerable talent.

Premiership Pals:

The squad will include Per Mertesacker, Mesut Özil and Lukas Podolski of Arsenal, and André Schürrle from Chelsea. In addition there's Jérôme Boateng (now Bayern Munich, once Manchester City), whose similarly ex-Premiership brother Kevin Prince Boateng plays for Ghana.

World Cup Previous:

As West Germany, they have won the trophy three times. In 1954 they came from behind to beat a hugely popular and talented Hungary in the final, while in 1974 they came from behind to beat a hugely popular and talented Holland in the final. At Italia 90 they beat Argentina in an ugly final game, the only goal a contentious penalty, finishing the match playing against nine bad-tempered men. They were also runners-up three times, in 1966, 1982 and 1986.

PORTUGAL

FIFA RANKING: 5   *World cup wins: 0*
Kit: Dark red shirts, dark red shorts, dark red socks.
World cup odds: 33-1 (=11th favourites)

POR

CRISTIANO AND THE BOYS ARE BY NO MEANS THE FIRST Portuguese to dream of ruling in Brazil. During the Peninsular War the Portuguese moved their royal court from Lisbon to Brazil, their colony, to keep themselves safe from the rampant forces of Napoleon – very much the Moriarty of invasion. They liked it so much that when the war was over they didn't want to go back. They tried creating a new country, the United Kingdom of Portugal, Brazil and the Algarves, to justify staying, but in the end revolution at home forced their hand. The Royals departed, leaving their son Prince Pedro as regent, and he promptly sided with the rebels and declared himself Emperor. Kids, eh...?

How they got there:

Portugal finished second in UEFA Group F, a point behind Russia, with home draws against Israel and Northern Ireland proving costly. Their playoff games with Sweden were billed as a shoot out between Cristiano Ronaldo and Zlatan Ibrahimovic, which Ronaldo won 4-2 on aggregate.

How will they do?

No metatarsals will be monitored with more anxiety than those of Cristiano Ronaldo. If he is at his best, the Real Madrid genius can be the difference against any opposition.

The Manager:

As a player, Paolo Bento won 35 caps, and was suspended by FIFA for five months for abusing match officials in the fracas at the Euro 2000 semi-final, which Portugal lost to France. As coach, he had more Euro semi-final heartbreak in 2012, losing on penalties to Spain.

Watch out for:

You wouldn't call Portugal a one-man team, but when Cristiano Ronaldo dragged them single-footedly past Sweden in November they almost looked like one. When he first came to Manchester United he seemed to be a one-trick pony, the only question being how many step-overs he would attempt before losing the ball. Nowadays, though, he has it all – pace, power, ball control, judgement, leadership, and that deadly swerving dipping free kick where he strikes the ball right on the valve – and he is vying only with Lionel Messi for the title of best player in the world.

Premiership Pals:

There's really only Nani of Man. United. In addition you will be able to spot Cristiano Ronaldo (Real Madrid, but once Manchester United), Helder Postiga (former Spurs big money striker, now playing for Lazio) and Raul Meireles (Fenerbahce, formerly of Liverpool and Chelsea).

World Cup Previous:

Portugal's best World Cup performance is their third place in 1966, when they lost to England in the semi-final, and late legend Eusebio won the Golden Boot. They reached the semi-final again in 2006, having taken revenge on England on the way, but lost to a Zinedine Zidane penalty. Last time they made it into the last 16 with two goalless draws and a 7-0 gubbing of North Korea, but a single David Villa goal saw Spain through at their expense.

GHANA

FIFA RANKING: 24   World cup wins: 0
Kit: All white.

World cup odds: 150-1 (=18th favourites)

GHA

I N 1957, AS PART OF GHANA'S INDEPENDENCE CELEBRA-
TIONS, new President Kwame Nkrumah invited the world's
most famous footballer, Stanley Matthews, to visit. Sir Stanley,
then 42, guested for Accra Hearts of Oak, and was crowned King of
Football in a strange-looking ceremony, wearing native robes and
seated rather self-consciously on a large throne carved out of wood
and ivory in the shape of an elephant, a football beneath each san-
dal-shod foot. In later life, Matthews coached a young black South
African team called Sir Stan's Men, taking them on tour to Rio de
Janeiro.

How they got there:

Ghana topped African Group D, losing just one game. Their
subsequent playoff with Egypt was over by the halfway point, as they
thrashed their fancied opponents 6-1 in Kumasi. They lost the return
2-1, but it didn't matter. Asamoah Gyan scored six qualifying goals.

How will they do?

Ghana reached the final of the 2014 African Nations Championship,
which they lost on penalties to Libya. Having gone out of the last
World Cup on penalties as well, Ghana will be hoping that no further
twelve-yard heartbreak awaits them in Brazil

The Manager:

James Kwesi Appiah has spent time picking up tips from Roberto Mancini at Manchester City's training sessions. He has been assistant coach to Milovan Rajevac in 2010, and he managed Ghana's under-23s to gold at the 2011 All Africa Games.

Watch out for:

Marseille midfielder Andre Ayew has been described as "world class" by Appiah. Born in France, because his father (former Ghana captain Abedi Pele) was playing for Lille at the time, Andre Ayew made his debut for Ghana at the age of 17 against Senegal. His brothers Ibrahim and Jordan are also Ghanaian internationals.

Premiership Pals:

Michael Essien left Chelsea for the second time to join AC Milan in January. Derek Boateng has been at Fulham for a season. Emmanuel Frimpong, once of Arsenal now at Barnsley, played one qualifier. Sulley Muntari of AC Milan was once a big money signing by Portsmouth. Asamoah Gyan left Sunderland for the UAE. And Kevin Prince Boateng, once of Spurs and Portsmouth, is likely to come up against his brother Jérôme, who represents Germany.

World Cup Previous:

Ghana have appeared only at the two most recent tournaments. They made it to the second round in 2006 with wins over the Czech Republic and the USA, before bowing out to Brazil. In 2010 they reached the quarter finals, and a late late winner was heading goalwards until Uruguay's Luis Suarez punched it out. Asamoah Gyan missed the resulting penalty, and the Black Stars mucked up the penalty shoot out, which could have seen them becoming the first African side to make the semis.

USA

FIFA RANKING: 14   World cup wins: 0
Kit: All white.

World cup odds: 175-1 (=22nd favourites)

UNLIKE MOST OF THE COUNTRIES AT THE WORLD CUP, the USA wouldn't even begin to claim that soccerball was their favourite sport. Not when there's glorified rounders to watch, or that sort of crash-helmeted shoulder-padded forty-seven-a-side rugby they seem to like so much. The trouble with footy is that it's so hard to find gaps long enough to cram adverts for Coke into. They have a professional league, the MLS (Major League Soccer), which was founded in 1993 as part of the successful USA bid to host the 1994 World Cup. However, their franchise system is so baffling, with teams disappearing and re-emerging with a different name in a different place, that it's really hard to follow. David Beckham is apparently trying to start up a new team in Miami – maybe we can look out for them. For a year or two....

How they got there:

USA comfortably topped the CONCACAF qualifying process, well ahead of Costa Rica, Honduras and Mexico. Jozy Altidore grabbed four, comfortably more than in his first half-season for Sunderland.

How will they do?

They are in good shape. Recently they were on a run of 17 wins in 20 matches, which included victories over all their fellow CONCACAF qualifiers, plus South Korea and their top-seeded opponents here, Germany, who they turned over 4-3 in Washington D.C.

The Manager:

Jürgen Klinsmann, the VW-driving former-Spurs blonde belly-flop champion, will send his boys out against the home country he starred for and managed at previous tournaments. To add spice, the Germans are now managed by his protégé, Jogi Löw.

Watch out for:

Michael Bradley signed for Toronto FC from AS Roma in early 2014 for ten million bucks, and he will be loading the bullets for hotshot Jermaine Defoe. Bradley has been the key player in the recent successes of Klinsmann's team, with his box-to-box energy and his tireless work-rate driving them on. His success in the rôle of deep-lying creator has been credited with getting the best out of Jozy Altidore...

Premiership Pals:

Jozy Altidore (Sunderland), Tim Howard (Everton, Brad Guzan (Aston Villa), Geoff Cameron, Maurice Edu and Brek Shea (Stoke City), and Clint Dempsey, who has been back at his old club, Fulham, on loan from Seattle Sounders since January. There's also Eddie Johnson (DC United, formerly Fulham), Eric Lichaj (Nottingham Forest, formerly Aston Villa), and Stuart Holden, who played in the top flight for Bolton.

World Cup Previous:

The USA's best performance was third place in the very first tournament, when they lost (heavily) to Argentina in the semi-final. In 1950 they pulled off a shock 1-0 win over England in Belo Horizonte, then didn't qualify again until 1990. Hosts in 1994, they have been at every tournament since, their best run being in the Far East in 2002, when they were unlucky to lose to Germany in the quarter final. Revenge is on the cards...

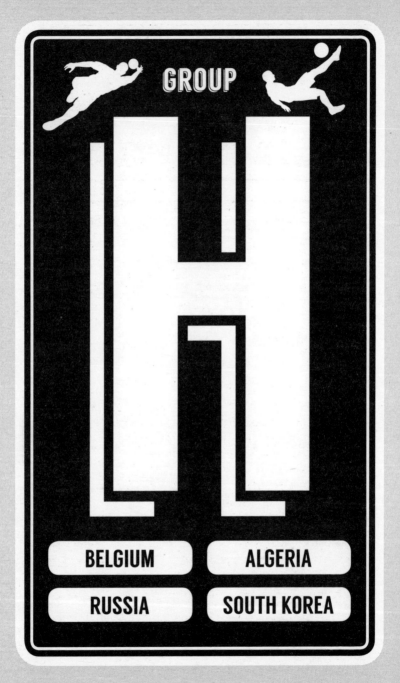

GROUP

H

BELGIUM

ALGERIA

RUSSIA

SOUTH KOREA

GROUP H

17 JUNE	17:00 ITV	BELO HORIZONTE
BELGIUM		ALGERIA

17 JUNE	23:00 BBC	CUIABA
RUSSIA		SOUTH KOREA

22 JUNE	17:00 BBC	RIO DE JANEIRO
BELGIUM		RUSSIA

22 JUNE	20:00 ITV	PORTO ALEGRE
SOUTH KOREA		ALGERIA

26 JUNE	21:00 ITV	SAO PAULO
SOUTH KOREA		BELGIUM

26 JUNE	21:00 ITV	CURITIBA
ALGERIA		RUSSIA

	W	D	L	F	A	Pts

133

BELGIUM

FIFA RANKING: 11   **World cup wins: 0**

Kit: Red shirts with yellow andblack trim, red shorts, red socks

World cup odds: 14-1 (5th favourites)

BEL

B ELGIUM ARE CURRENTLY ENJOYING A GOLDEN GENERATION, as evidenced by the presence of so many of their squad in our Premiership, players that England would welcome with open arms. They are strongly tipped to have a very good tournament, but it's not so very long ago that they were in the doldrums, with midfielder Steven Defour (of F.C. Porto) describing his own national team as "deadly sick". After qualifying for six straight World Cups between 1982 and 2002, they have not made it to a major tournament since – until now. Their supporters' belief has been severely tested – they famously only had one supporter at an away qualifier in Armenia – but their upcoming young generation finished fourth at the Olympics in Beijing, and are now arguably coming to fruition, as the form team in Europe.

How they got there:

Belgium topped UEFA Group A, nine whole points clear of the internecine squabble between Croatia and Serbia. They won all their away games, Thibaut Courtois kept six clean sheets, and Kevin de Bruyne top scored with four.

How will they do?

They could do very well, depending really on who they meet from Group G in the last 16. And remember, victory for Belgium is a victory for the Premiership. Kind of...

The Manager:

Marc Wilmots was a top international player, Belgium's leading World Cup goalscorer, and also a politician, sitting in the Belgian Senate for two years representing the centre-right Mouvement Réformateur, before deciding that politics wasn't for him.

Watch out for:

If this Belgian all-star team has a stand-out player it is surely Eden Hazard. His chances of being picked out by Pele would be improved by the presence of his lookalike younger brother Thorgan in the team – Pele's selection of Nicky Butt in 2002 was surely influenced by him thinking that Butt and Paul Scholes were the same player. Hazard (senior)'s undeniable ball skills have been turning more and more efficiently into goals lately, and he could be the star of the tournament.

Premiership Pals:

Loads. Simon Mignolet (Liverpool), Romelu Lukaku and Kevin Mirallas (Everton), Vincent Kompany (Manchester City), Eden Hazard and Kevin de Bruyne (Chelsea), Moussa Dembélé, Jan Vertonghen and Nacer Chadli (Spurs), Marouane Fellaini (Manchester United), Christian Benteke (Aston Villa), Thomas Vermaelen (Arsenal), and Roland Lamah (Swansea City). Thibaut Courtois of Atletico Madrid is on loan from Chelsea.

World Cup Previous:

Belgium's previous "golden generation" reached the semi-final in 1986, losing to Argentina (c.f. that famous photograph of Maradona faced with half a dozen scared-looking Belgian defenders). Perhaps they took inspiration from their World Cup song De Rode Duivels gaan naar Mexico. Otherwise they regularly make it through to the second stage – David Platt famously did for them in 1990, while in 1994 they beat the Dutch and lost to Germany.

SOUTH KOREA

FIFA RANKING: 53 *World cup wins: 0*
Kit: Red shirts, blue shorts, red socks
World cup odds: 350-1 (26th favourites)

KOR

SOUTH KOREA HAD A THRILLING RUN TO THE SEMI-FINAL at the 2002 World Cup, and to be fair they had several things going for them: the support of hyper-excited fanatical crowds, a top foreign coach in Guus Hiddink, and – crucially – the fact that they were utterly brilliant at penalties, simply because every K-League game that finishes in a draw goes to a shoot-out. So when South Korea and Spain drew their quarter-final in Gwangju the hosts had a distinct advantage. Lee Woon-Jae, their keeper, had won all seven of his K-League shootouts that year, and Hong Myung-Bo, now their coach, won the match with the kick of an absolute specialist, turning his foot so far that it almost seemed to be pointing backwards as he steered the ball into the top corner.

How they got there:

Perennial qualifiers, South Korea made heavy weather of it this time, squeaking past Uzbekistan on goal difference in AFC Group A to finish second behind Iran. Lee Keun-Ho bagged six qualifying goals.

How will they do?

South Korea are not in the best of form, and their squeaky-bum qualification cost coach Choi Kang-Hee his job (turning up for a press conference in an Uzbekistan shirt didn't help either). They have regularly lost friendlies against fellow qualifiers since, and could struggle to go through.

The Manager:

Hong Myung-Bo is South Korea's most-capped player, and one of Asian football's all-time greats. He captained South Korea to fourth place in 2002, and was voted third in the Player of the Tournament poll. Took over after the 2014 qualifiers, in which the team did not impress.

Watch out for:

Kim Nam-Il became a star at the 2002 World Cup with his defensive displays alongside current manager Hong Myung-Bo. Guus Hiddink converted him from an attacking midfielder, and his tackling was so clean and effective that he earned the nickname "The Vacuum Cleaner". He was highly sought after by companies for adverts, and gained an unusually large female fan base, thanks partly to an on-off relationship with a celebrity television anchorwoman girlfriend, partly to his nickname.

Premiership Pals:

There's Ji Dong-Won and Ki Sung-Yueng of Sunderland. In addition, Lee Chung-Yong is a favourite at Bolton, and played in the Premiership for them, and Kim Do-Heon played for West Brom. Park Ji-Sung, formerly of Manchester United, has now retired, but nominated Kim Bo-Kyung of Cardiff as his successor in the South Korea number 7 shirt.

World Cup Previous:

South Korea appeared briefly in 1954, shipping 16 goals in two games, then not again until 1986. Since then, however, they have been regulars, and this will be their eighth straight tournament. Their best performance by far was in 2002, when, as co-hosts, they saw off Italy and Spain and went all the way to the semi-final, where they ran out of gas against the Germans. Made the last 16 in South Africa, losing to Uruguay.

ALGERIA

FIFA RANKING: 7   *World cup wins: 0*

Kit: White shirts with green trim, white shorts, white socks.

World cup odds: 1000-1 (29th favourites)

ALGERIA'S FIRST EVER GAME AT THE WORLD CUP, IN 1982, pitted them against the European Champions West Germany – and they beat them 2-1. Algeria lost then to Austria and beat Chile in their third game, which meant that they would qualify for the next round unless the Germans beat Austria by one or two goals the next day, in which case both European teams would progress. Horst Hrubesch put the West Germans ahead on ten minutes... and then nothing else happened, no attacks, no tackles, no shots. For eighty minutes. This disgraceful collusion – dubbed El Anschluss in Spain – was widely condemned, but there was nothing that FIFA or anyone else could do. Which is why, children, the last games in each group are now played simultaneously

How they got there:

Algeria coasted through the minnow pool that was African Group H, past Mali, Benin and Rwanda, and then won a two-legged playoff against surprise package Burkina Faso. It finished 3-3 on aggregate, but Algeria slipped through on away goals. Islam Slimani contributed five goals.

How will they do?

It is difficult to tell whether Algeria have any form, because they have not really played any testing opposition since drawing with Ivory Coast over a year ago. Probably rightly regarded as the group underdogs.

The Manager:

Vahid "Vaha" Halilhodži is a Bosnian, who played international football for Yugoslavia, and earned a reputation as a "tactical scientist" while coaching in France. He led the Ivory Coast to qualification for the last World Cup, but was sacked before the tournament itself.

Watch out for:

Islam Slimani is a big, strong centre forward with a good scoring record of better than a goal every other game for Algeria. The fact that Sam Allardyce was interested in him during the January transfer window should give you some idea of his strengths. Slimani moved from Algerian club football to Sporting Lisbon last summer, and hasn't really been able to force his way into regular first team action, but he has caught the eye for his country.

Premiership Pals:

Adlène Guedioura, of Crystal Palace, has also played for Nottingham Forest and Wolves, and won both clubs' Goal of the Season awards in the same season, which takes a bit of doing. Madjid Bougherra played in Charlton Athletic's last Premiership season, and also for Sheffield Wednesday. Rafik Djebbour (Nottingham Forest) and Essa d Belkalem (Watford) play in the Championship

World Cup Previous:

Algeria have appeared in three World Cup tournaments, in 1982, 1986 and 2010, without ever progressing beyond the first group stage. Their best run was undoubtedly in 1982, when they won two matches (including a notable victory over West Germany), only to be denied by the disgraceful collusion between the Germans and the Austrians. In 1986 they drew with Northern Ireland and last time with England, which provided their only points since then.

RUSSIA

FIFA RANKING: 15 *World cup wins: 0*
Kit: Red shirts, red shorts, red socks.

World cup odds: 66-1 (14th favourites)

RUS

R USSIA WON'T HAVE TO QUALIFY NEXT TIME – THEY will be the hosts, the first Eastern European country to stage a World Cup. So how did they beat England to get the 2018 gig? Well, Moscow now boasts more billionaires than any other city in the world, thanks to Russian oil, and many of these guys take more than a passing interest in football. Jérôme Valcke of FIFA vehemently denied that bribery had played any part in the Russian (and Qatari) bids, saying that they had merely used "financial muscle to lobby for support". We, on the other hand, used David Beckham, Prince William and David Cameron. That won't be the end of the controversy, even though there are likely to be fewer participants speaking out about Russia's arcane attitudes to homosexuality than there were at, say, the ice dancing in Sochi.

How they got there:

Russia finished top of UEFA Group F, one point ahead of Portugal. Each won the home game against the other 1-0, but Russia's record against the smaller teams was slightly better, despite a defeat by Northern Ireland. Aleksandr Kerzhakov scored five goals for them.

How will they do?

Likely to be organised to the point of rigidity, Russia should figure in the knockout stage.

The Manager:

Under Fabio Capello, England qualified with ease for the 2010 World Cup. Once at the tournament, however, Capello came unstuck, imposing a strict and unpopular pseudo-military regime at the England training camp, and dismissing the tactical input of senior players. Maybe his style will suit the Russians better...

Watch out for:

With an impressive 181 goals in 410 games Zenit St Petersburg's Aleksandr Kerzhakov is the most prolific goalscorer in the history of Russian football. Of course, this is a bit like when English pundits say so-and-so is the most something "in the history of the Premiership", thus simply not counting Gary Lineker, or Bobby Charlton, or Dixie Dean. Russia in its present form dates back only to 1992, and the Russian Premier League was founded in 2001.

Premiership Pals:

Pavel Pogrebnyak has played in the Premier League for Fulham and Reading. Lokomotiv Moscow's Diniyar Bilyaletdinov had three seasons with Everton, while Yuri Zhirkov played for Chelsea. Former Gunner Andrey Arshavin has not been selected since saying that if people felt let down by Russia's showing at Euro 2012 "that was their problem".

World Cup Previous:

As Russia, they have qualified twice before, but failed to progress beyond the group stage either at USA 94 or in the Far East in 2002, where they lost a grudge game against Japan, with whom they are still technically at war over some disputed islands. As the Soviet Union they were quarter-finalists four times in a row from 1958-70, going on to the semi in 1966, but they were disqualified in 1974 for refusing to play Chile.

SECOND ROUND

SR1	28 JUNE	17:00	BELO HORIZONTE
A1			B2
SR2	28 JUNE	21:00	RIO DE JANEIRO
C1			D2
SR5	30 JUNE	17:00	BRASILIA
E1			F2
SR6	30 JUNE	21:00	PORTO ALEGRE
G1			H2
SR3	29 JUNE	17:00	FORTALEZA
B1			A2
SR4	29 JUNE	21:00	RECIFE
D1			C2
SR7	01 JULY	17:00	SAO PAULO
F1			E2
SR8	01 JULY	21:00	SALVADOR
H1			G2

QUARTER FINALS

QF2	04 JULY	21:00	FORTALEZA
WINNER SR1			
WINNER SR2			

QF1	04 JULY	17:00	RIO DE JANEIRO
WINNER SR5			
WINNER SR6			

QF4	05 JULY	21:00	SALVADOR
WINNER SR3			
WINNER SR4			

QF3	05 JULY	17:00	BRASILIA
WINNER SR7			
WINNER SR8			

SEMI FINALS & FINAL

SF1   08 JULY   21:00   BELO HORIZONTE

WINNER QF1

WINNER QF2

FINAL   13 JULY   20:00   RIO DE JANEIRO

SF2   09 JULY   21:00   SAO PAULO

WINNER QF3

WINNER QF4

3RD/4TH PLAY-OFF   12 JULY   21:00   BRASILIA

HIT THE HEADLINES

England star Wayne Rooney makes plenty of headlines, doesn't he? However, the only real pun you can make on his surname is LOONEY, and what editor is going to risk the litigation grief? So they usually shorten it to ROO – IT'S UP TO ROO, IT HAD TO BE ROO, ROO ONLY SCORE TWICE, etc.

Nowadays the ROO headline is a modern classic. One glorious day Wayne will been asked onto BBC1's prime time genealogy show, and they'll be able to crank out ROO DO ROO THINK ROO ARE?

Down in Brazil I suppose ROO DE JANEIRO is a possible, but given that England's first game is way way up the Amazon, where the locals get about the place in little canoes, I am expecting a photo op at some point with Wayno sat in one. At which point some bright spark will come up with:

ROO ROO ROO YOUR BOAT!

THE HOW TO PICK A 2ND TEAM FLOW CHART

Are they likely to actually go home before England, thus rendering the choice moot?

YES
(although this is clearly a hostage to fortune that could come back and bite me)

NO

Cameroon, Costa Rica, Iran, Nigeria, Algeria, Greece, Japan, Honduras

Do they have a nice kit that I could buy a replica shirt of and wear at social events during the world cup, such as at a Brazilian-style churrasco?

CHRIST NO, it would be social suicide

Germany

NO

YES

Croatia (migraine-inducing checkerboard) **USA** (just white, no interesting stars and stripes motif, nothing. Dull.) **Bosnia & Herzegovina** (also just white, with a bit of blue Euro-trim) **Ghana** (also just white) **Russia** (red now, apparently, having been white and blue before. Confused.) **Switzerland** (yawn...) **Chile** (red, about as interesting as Orient)

YES, definitely, it's a timeless classic

YES, Could probably carry it off

Will they stomp all over most opposition, thus giving me the vicarious validation that England so rarely provide?

Brazil, Netherlands, Italy, Spain, Uruguay, Australia

Argentina, France, Colombia, Belgium, Portugal, Mexico, Ivory Coast, Ecuador, South Korea

YES

MAYBE

NO

Brazil, Germany *(how did they get back in again?)* Spain, Argentina, Netherlands, Italy

Uruguay, France, Colombia, Belgium, Portugal

Can they actually go all the way, and keep my interest alive right to the final?

Australia, Mexico, Ivory Coast, Ecuador, South Korea

NO

YES

Brazil, Spain, Germany, Argentina, Netherlands, Italy, France, Portugal

Uruguay, Belgium, Colombia

Would you back them in a penalty shoot out?

YES

NO → **Netherlands** (always cock it up), **Italy** (mentally fragile), **France** (combustible), **Portugal** (only Ronaldo will score and they'll leave him till last so he may not even get to have a go)

Brazil, Spain, Germany (ruthless), **Argentina** (lucky)

Is there any lingering resentment over previously having been at war with this country?

OH MY GOODNESS ME YES → **Germany** (1914-18, 1939-45, and Manuel Neuer conning the referee about the Frank Lampard 'goal' in 2010) **Argentina** (Malvinas. I mean, Falklands, and Maradona's "Hand of God")

NO → **Brazil**

NOT REALLY → **Spain** (the Armada was a long time ago)

What sort of football are they likely to play? **S**ilky **S**amba-**S**tyle **S**unshine footy? Or **T**edious **T**ime-consuming **T**iki-**T**aka?

TTTT → Spain

SSSS → **Brazil**

HOW TO PICK A 2ND TEAM (IF YOU DON'T WANT TO SUPPORT BRAZIL)

GROUP A

BRAZIL • MEXICO • CROATIA • CAMEROON

Well, **Brazil**, obviously. And that's the thing, isn't it? It's just a bit obvious. The colour, the samba-style support, the *jogo bonito*. They are such strong favourites that they will appeal to the weak-willed, those who will only support a team if it has a massive unfair advantage over everyone they play. Chelsea fans, in other words.

Following **Mexico** offers definite prop and costume benefits. A sombrero is an easy fun signifier, and you can use it to keep crisps in during games. Then there is the poncho (Clint Eastwood-style), the Zapata moustache (Graham Gooch-style), the not shaving and calling everyone "Gringo!" – that *never* gets tired. On the downside you could find yourself saying: "¡Ándale! ¡Ándale! ¡Arriba! ¡Arriba!" when ordering drinks or food, which will get you a slap sooner or later.

If you like dressing up smart to watch your international football, then following **Croatia** gives you the perfect excuse. The necktie originates from the cravat worn by 17th-century Croat soldiers, and the name 'cravat' comes from the name of the country – Hrvatska.

Choosing **Cameroon** may just put you in prime bragging position if they pull off a shock defeat of Brazil, making you look like a mystical football seer. Like Alan Hansen. However they have a German manager who doesn't know anything about African football, may very well lose all their games, and as they are in Group A may once again be the first team on the plane home.

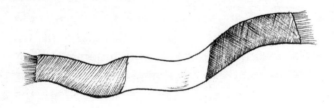

GROUP B

SPAIN • NETHERLANDS • CHILE • AUSTRALIA

Spain have a decent chance of going all the way. If you like Man City it will almost be like watching them play – Silva, out wide to Navas, crosses in to Negredo – *goal*! And if you think possession stats rather than goals should decide games then Spain are the boys for you. There is, though, a very real danger that they will send you to sleep during matches, with their endlessly hypnotic tippy-tappy shifting the ball sideways 35 yards out, without anyone daring to take the plunge and actually have a pop at goal.

Going Dutch for a month has a definite appeal to the connoisseur. Those orange **Netherlands** shirts are extremely good-looking, as football kits go. Name-checking their tradition of total football will make you look like you know what you are talking about. This selection also comes with some interesting cheeseboard options, and a range of decent lagers. Not to mention a relaxed attitude to other relaxing methods of relaxation. They do, however, have a distressingly flaky record when it comes to the old penalty shoot-outs...

In **Chile's** favour is their fantastic *Mouse That Roared* national anthem, whose twists and turns are impossible for the mere layman to predict, but the Chileans really *really* go for it, with none of the bashful diffidence we reserve for that rather dull song we do about the Queen. The footage of the legendary Ivan Zamorano bellowing this at France 98 is a thing of splendour. Learn this song, amaze your friends and relatives...

Surely it's too soon, after the winter's debacles, to generate any enthusiasm for **Australia**? Just think of David Warner's face. If you do take the plunge, well, the green and gold shirt is distinctive, and likely to get you served quickly in most London pubs, especially in the Earl's Court area. And a hat with corks is always fun. And maybe you could enjoy a stubby or two, and some of those tasty-looking Aussie snacks, such as you see the celebs munching on that jungle show...

GROUP C

COLOMBIA • IVORY COAST • GREECE • JAPAN

Colombia have a nice summery yellow shirt. Becoming a vocal supporter could make people think you are connected in some way to drugs cartels, and you might finally start getting the respect at work that you so richly deserve. The downside is that it could lead to cavity searches, and nobody wants that. And that Gabriel Garcia Marquez novel sticking out of your pocket? There's no way you're finishing that...

Ivory Coast's orange shirt is also attractive, and if you make yourself a convincing enough elephant mask (their nickname is *Les Éléphants*) you could score some free buns. There are some familiar names to spot, especially for Chelsea and Manchester City fans, and it is probably the last opportunity to cheer on Didier Drogba's marvellous athleticism and drive.

There are many restaurants where you will be welcomed with open arms, and who knows, maybe a complimentary kebab, if you show up in a **Greece** shirt. They may even let you smash crockery all over the place if the team win, or if they lose, or if a good song comes on the radio, or if one of their daughters has become engaged. If they concede a goal you can say "Balalaikas!" as if you are swearing, and people may find this amusing the first three or four times.

Japanese restaurants may well have the telly on, but will they have the **Japan** games on, or any Japanese football fans working there or eating there? Then there's the business of the raw fish. If they'd just slap some batter on it, deep fry it, and bung it in some newspaper with some chips, then I could see the attraction...

GROUP D

URUGUAY • ITALY • COSTA RICA • ENGLAND

You probably won't want to pick a Group D team as your second team if you are an England fan, although if England go out you could follow the progress of their conquerors in a wistful "if only" sort of way. **Uruguay** have a nice retro pale blue kit to wear, but the question of whether or not to support them is mainly going to be determined by your attitude to Luis Suárez. Either he is one of the most exciting players in the world, or a slightly effeminate short-arsed Freddie Mercury lookalike, liable to fall over if an opponent exhales nearby, or to help his team progress by handling the ball in the last minute of a key game, like he did against Ghana last time.

Fans of cynical referee-manipulation may be strongly drawn to this next option, but following **Italy** is liable to be a nervy business. They are under so much pressure from the fans they already have, many of whom have been stockpiling fruit for some time in preparation for welcoming the team home early at the airport, that the temptation to park the bus becomes overwhelming for them. The *azzurri* shirt is a football classic, though, and Italian nights of pizza and pasta would be a treat. You may need the team to get through several rounds to check out all the wines, although if Montepulciano and Valpolicella don't send you to sleep, then Prandelli and Pirlo might.

On the face of it, **Costa Rica** would be on odd choice for a second team, but as a nation they have a peaceful, cheery outlook which sits well with their status as tournament underdogs. If your idea of a fun-packed ninety minutes is nail-biting backs-to-the-wall defending by a team whose star player is the goalkeeper, punctuated by occasional bursts of harum-scarum long-legged counter-attacking, then maybe the Ticos are for you.

Calling Scots, Welshmen, and Irishmen everywhere – it's only two short years since we all got behind Team GB at the London Olympics, so surely you can find it in your hearts to cheer on Roy and the boys? We all got behind Chris Hoy, Ryan Giggs and Andy Murray every bit as much as we loved Bradley Wiggins and Jessica Ennis (well, perhaps not quite as much as we loved Jessica Ennis...). So come on, how about it? **England** will surely welcome casual support from other nations, too. What about South Africans, for example? They haven't qualified this time, but they must have a soft spot for our cricket team, since it has almost as many South Africans in it as theirs does, so maybe some of that residual affection will be transferable...?

GROUP E

SWITZERLAND • FRANCE • HONDURAS • ECUADOR

It is going to be hard to enjoy **Switzerland** doing well, since we will be playing them later this year in qualifying for Euro 2016, and the vague interest we had in them once because an obscure Brit was their manager has long since worn off (whatever happened to that guy? Ray Hodgburn, something like that...?). If you choose the Swiss you'd better like the Orson Welles quote – "In Switzerland, they had brotherly love and five hundred years of democracy and peace, and what did they produce? The cuckoo clock!" – because you are going to hear it a lot.

France are our neighbours, after all, and if you are a Newcastle fan you practically support France already. The blue shirt goes with pretty much anything, and it would be an excuse to buy lots of soft cheeses and long crusty loaves, maybe get a basket on the front of your bike. And if you have a holiday house in the Dordogne then it might be a good way to stop your neighbours there and local tradespeople from hating your guts. But don't bet on it.

I am going to want **Honduras** to do well, not just because they are the rankest of rank outsiders at this World Cup and there's something very British about rooting for them because of that, but also because they have Carlos Costly playing for them, and I want him to come to the Premiership. With his name he is like a one-man walking satire on modern football.

Ecuador are yet another South American yellow-shirted team, and they might reward your secondary support simply because they are so under-rated. They actually out-qualified Uruguay, so they might have a chance of causing genuine upsets, which might make you look like a pundit-genius...

GROUP F

ARGENTINA • BOSNIA & HERZEGOVINA • NIGERIA • IRAN

As far as **Argentina** is concerned there are fairly weighty historical arguments against choosing them as your second team. There's the whole Falklands/ Malvinas thing, as well as the Maradona handball thing, and if you get vocal in your support of them in a pub then you will certainly find out in pretty short order whether there are any squaddies around. On the other hand, though, there's Messi...

The problem with sticking up for **Bosnia and Herzegovina** is that very few football chants are designed for teams with nine syllables. In fact the only one that seems to fit the name neatly is the one that usually features the words "You're going to get your ****ing head kicked in!", which may end up causing more trouble than it's worth.

Nigeria have a nice green shirt, which is a plus point, and they have been doing fairly well recently, so you might get a bit of mileage out of them. Plus it was ours until 1960, and they're still in the Commonwealth, so if they do well the Queen will be chuffed. She's pretty much obliged to be.

The main drawback about becoming an **Iran** supporter is that if you are going to get into it properly you might just have to stop drinking for a month. For some of you that wouldn't be a problem, of course, and for others I dare say it would be a really good idea. Non-alcoholic beer, though, well, I've never really got on with that.

GROUP G

GERMANY • USA • PORTUGAL • GHANA

On the face of it, there are sound reasons for selecting **Germany** as your second team to follow. They are certainly in with a chance of doing well, even though this is a tough group, and the beer is definitely a factor. Go and watch a game in one of the big Bavarian beerhouses, with massive foaming steins brought to you by lasses in dirndls and fellows in lederhosen (or vice versa), and it is Oktoberfest all year round. Chances are they'll keep their cool in a penalty shoot out, too. I don't think I could bring myself to do it, though...

I am rather drawn to the idea of supporting the **United States**. Usually Americans are quite triumphalist about sport – about everything – but they're not actually all that good at 'soccerball', so their fans have a reasonable sense of proportion. And the way they and their commentators talk about the game is hilarious. When a corner comes into the area, they hope that their striker will 'top-body the sphere into the onion bag'. If he hits the post they will call that 'a pole shot'. If it bounces into the keeper's territory it's 'in the wheelhouse'. Winning the ball back is called 'bulldogging'. Almost any stupid thing you can make up they already do. It's hilarious.

Rooting for **Portugal** is basically rooting for Cristiano Ronaldo, so dominant a personality is the wet-look Real Madrid pants model. So if you are impressed by the step-overs, and the preening, and the flawless gleaming teeth, then maybe this is the choice for you. If, however, you'd secretly like to see him fall on his face, crunched by some no-name destroyer from a minnow nation, then maybe not.

Ghana had a good run last time, and could be the team that carries the hopes of a continent once again. We don't really do that in Europe, do we, support the other European teams against the other continents? Anyway, if you love the warmth of the African sun on your soul, then maybe Ghana are for you.

GROUP H

ALGERIA • SOUTH KOREA • RUSSIA • BELGIUM

It is not that easy to make a case for **Algeria**, unfortunately, but if they do get it together and sneak second place, then they might get to play the Germans in the last 16. Those who remember the disgraceful carry-on of 1982 might hop on board the Algeria bandwagon in the hope of enjoying some sort of ghastly karmic revenge being visited upon the villains of that particular piece.

Then there is **South Korea**, who seem unlikely to attract people's enthusiasm in the numbers they managed in their run to the semi-final on home turf back in 2002. I'm afraid many will steer clear for fear of upsetting a dog lover in the family, or a fan of M*A*S*H, who remembers what happened to that nice Henry...

Russia offers all sorts of possibilities for dressing up, although Soviet-style greatcoats and fur hats may ultimately be quite hard work at that summer barbecue. The way the Russians have been carrying on this spring, it's perhaps as well that we knocked Ukraine out, and the publicity surrounding the Putin administration's attitude to homosexuality, which seems at odds with the Leader's own fondness for stripping to the waist and oiling his pecs, might cause people to tut at you and ask you what you think you are doing supporting Russia, which would be tiresome.

Belgium, however, is another story, and I can see a lot of people developing a soft spot for them. They're small enough to count as underdogs – which Brits love, obviously – but they also have a lot of really fine players, many of whom are very familiar from *Match of the Day*, and could spring a few surprises the longer the tournament goes on. And you can easily pick up a Fellaini wig. A downside for some people might be having to have mayonnaise on your chips instead of ketchup, but I happen to prefer mayonnaise anyway...

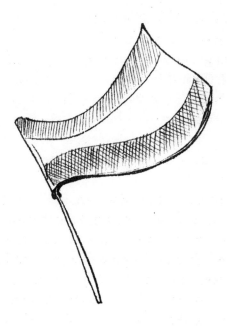

WORLD CUP SKILLS #3

The Ardiles Rainbow Flick

No question, pocket-sized Ossie Ardiles of Argentina was one of the most eye-catching stars of the 1978 World Cup – compact, tricky, and able to pass the ball through the eye of a needle, he was the man who made the champions tick. The trademark piece of individual skill that set Ossie apart was regularly shown off during warm-ups, but he didn't use it in an actual match until he played for the Allies against Germany in *Escape to Victory* three years later (or thirty-eight years earlier, depending how you look at it).

To pull this off, do as follows: step over the ball with your left foot, and with your right foot hug the ball up to just above your left heel. As you run forward, your momentum should enable you to flick the ball high into the air with your left heel, and if you are as good as Ossie used to be, then the ball will loop up over your head and into your stride, where you will control it and sprint effortlessly onwards. If you are not as good as Ossie then there is a chance that you will topple forwards on your face while the ball squirts backwards a couple of feet.

One man who actually did use the Ardiles High Heeler successfully to utterly bamboozle actual defences in not one but two World Cup matches in 2002 is pony-tailed boy wonder Ilhan Mansiz of Turkey, but since Ardiles got there first, and did it in an (albeit fictional) game against the Germans, and Pele was watching, and Bobby Moore, and Michael Caine, then it will forever bear his name. Mansiz will just have to dry his eyes with his own trademark tissues.

WORLD CUP MOVIE NIGHT

Here's an idea you can get the whole family behind. So sling half a cow on the *churrasco* (**p.46**), mix yourself a *caipirinha* (**p.186**), dim the lights, and press 'play'. But what movie to choose? Try the ones below, for starters...

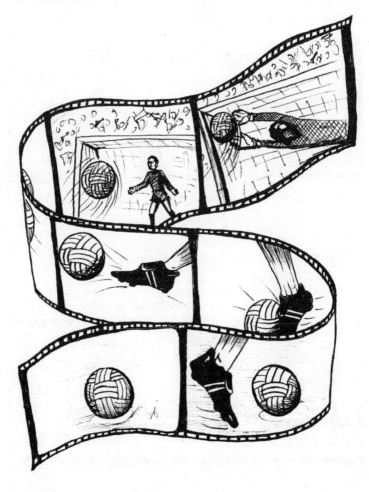

ONE NIGHT IN TURIN (2010)

Evocative documentary about Italia 90, when there were still hooligans, and England had a team that was good enough to compete with the best. Enjoy yourself like a 1990 England fan by shuffling slowly to the railway station surrounded by armed police. Or enjoy yourself like Gazza, by putting on false breasts and shoving someone's face into a cake, and then chucking the cake into a swimming pool.

ESCAPE TO VICTORY (1981)

Wartime kickball hokum featuring at least three people who actually won the World Cup. Enjoy yourself like these guys by deliberately breaking your mate's arm so Sylvester Stallone can play in goal (actually, no, don't), or by running around a football pitch in 1970s gear pretending it's 1944 just to confound the Nazis. Maybe not one for a movie night, though, because it'll probably be on next Sunday afternoon, or the Sunday after.

MIKE BASSETT: ENGLAND MANAGER (2001)

Good fun, and it's all to do with a World Cup in Brazil, so in many ways perfect. To my mind the best joke was actually in the spin-off television series, when Bassett is manager of a failing club sponsored by the waste removal department of a Merseyside council, which means the shirts bear the legend "Wirral Rubbish".

KICKING AND SCREAMING (2005)

Wanting to show up his over-competitive father, Will Ferrell becomes coach of his son's little league soccer team. I lost

the will to live about halfway through that last sentence...
If you liked *Anchorman*, why don't you watch that again?

AN EVENING WITH GARY LINEKER (1994)
I should declare an interest here, as I co-wrote this with Arthur Smith, based on our stage play about a group of people watching the Italia 90 semi-final in their hotel room in Majorca. It has Clive Owen in it, and Martin Clunes, and Gary Lineker (who was secretly wearing slippers because he'd broken a toe).

THE CUP (1999)
Students at a remote Tibetan monastery are on a mission to discover a television so they can watch the 1998 World Cup. Buddhism is their philosophy, soccer is their religion – see what they did there?

SHAOLIN SOCCER (2001)
An ex-pro soccer player hooks up with a shaolin kung fu student, and they bring his martial arts skills to bear on the football – sorry, *soccer* – pitch. Try to enjoy the World Cup like these fellows and you are probably going to end up in jail. Or at least facing a lengthy stadium ban, like Shaolin Pardew.

BRAZIL (1985)
Terry Gilliam's Kafkaesque vision of a future dogged with malfunctioning gadgetry and judicial torture is probably not going to be much use, come to think of it. If you want to see a film about football set in Brazil, then you'd be better off with...

LA GRAN FINAL (2006)

In which three disparate groups of people in three different parts of the world battle the odds to try and watch
the 2002 World Cup final between Brazil and Germany.
One group lives on a Mongolian steppe, another in Sa-
haran Nigeria, and the third in a remote part of the Amazonian rain forest. This last group's television breaks, and
they run around desperately until they find some American timber men who are ravaging their homeland, and
watch it with them.

SIXTY SIX (2006)

A boy's bar mitzvah coincides with the England v West
Germany 1966 World Cup final. It's another film about how
difficult it is for the characters to watch the football, and it
is really frustrating right up to the point where the boy and
his Dad race to Wembley and sneak in for the end.

NO HIDING PLACE (1973)

Not a movie, but a classic episode of *Whatever Happened
to the Likely Lads*, in which Bob and Terry try desperately
not to find out the score of a England qualifier before the
highlights are broadcast in the evening. It's just terrific,
and you could bung it on before the main film like an
old-style supporting feature. Enjoy the World Cup like
Messrs Ferris and Collier by not watching a match live, and
then trying to get to the highlights without being told
the score by one of the thousands of media outlets that
are desperate to do so. A much taller order today than
in 1973.

FOOD AND DRINK

Feijoada

Feijoada is a black bean-and-meat stew often described as the national dish of Brazil. It originated among the slave population, when Brazil was a Portuguese colony. Their masters would give them cheap rice and beans to eat, along with the unwanted leftover parts of the pig such as the feet, nose, ears and tail, and this cheerful chuck-everything-in stew is the result.

YOU WILL NEED:

1lb (450g) dry black beans
4 tablespoons olive oil
1lb (450g) pork shoulder cut into chunks, or else pork trimmings if you want to go trad
2 large onions, sliced
1 head of garlic, peeled and chopped
1lb *carne seca* or corned beef (if you prefer), cut into chunks
1/2lb fresh sausage, maybe chorizo or Italian sausage, whichever you like
1lb smoked sausage of your choice, or smoked pork ribs if you prefer
1 smoked ham hock or shank
3-4 bay leaves
1 can (411g) of crushed tomatoes
Vegetables (kale, potatoes, carrots, okra, pumpkin, chayote, banana – you choose), white rice

About 5 hours (most of which is waiting – actual preparation takes about a quarter of an hour)

WHAT YOU DO:

1. Pour boiling water over the black beans and let them sit while you get the rest of the stew ready.

2. Heat the olive oil in a large pot over medium heat, and brown the pork shoulder. Then remove the meat, set aside, and brown the onions in the pot, stirring occasionally. When they are done add salt and the garlic, and sauté for another couple of minutes.

3. Pop back the pork, add the other meats, and enough water to cover. Add the bay leaves, cover, and bring to a simmer, then cook gently for an hour.

4. Drain the black beans and add them to the stew. Simmer gently for another 90 minutes (maybe while one of the early evening games is on) until the beans are tender.

5. Add the tomatoes, and salt if needed. Simmer, uncovered, until the meat begins to fall off the ham hock (or shank), which could take another 2-3 hours.

6. Serve with white rice, hot sauce, a bit of dunking bread, and whatever vegetables you like. A typical accompaniment in Brazil would be collard greens.

This lot will serve about ten of you. Or five of you twice. Or two of you, on and off, for most of the group stages.

Enjoy.

QUIZ #2

Q1:   Who was the oldest player to score a goal for England in a World Cup finals match?

Q2:   Which three England players have been shown a red card during a World Cup finals match?

Q3:   Which colour shirts did Benito Mussolini insist the Italian players wear during the 1938 World Cup?

Q4:   Who was England's number 19 at the 1990 World Cup?

Q5:   Why was the ball changed at half time in the 1930 World Cup final?

Q6:   Which four players have been members of an England World Cup finals squad whilst belonging to a club in Scotland?

Q7:   Who ended up with the match ball after the 1966 World Cup final?

Q8:   Who was the first substitute used by England at a World Cup finals, replacing Keith Newton against Romania in 1970?

Q9:   Who are the only two British players to score in three World Cups?

Q10: Who were the goalscorers in the 1986 World Cup final?

Q11: What was the name of the octopus in the Sea Life Centre in Oberhausen, Germany, who was all over the news in 2010 predicting the results of World Cup matches?

Q12: When FIFA faced a(nother) corruption scandal in 2011, Sepp Blatter's solution was to propose a three-man "Council of Wisdom" to clean up the organisation. Who were the three wise men?

Q13: Who was England's number 9 at the 1986 World Cup?

Q14: During a World Cup match in 1982 the German keeper Harald Schumacher knocked out which French player with his backside?

Q15: Which four players have been sent off in a World Cup final?

Q16: In 1998, France became the sixth team to win the World Cup on home soil, who were the other five?

Q17: Who, in 1934, became the first African nation to play at a World Cup?

Q18: Which is the only stadium to have hosted two World Cup finals (until the Maracaná does similar in July)?

Q19: Who, in 1974, became the first country to be eliminated from a World Cup finals without losing a match?

Q20: The Brazilian referee of England's semi-final against West Germany at Italia 90 shared a surname with one of the England players – which one?

Answers on p.222

WORLD CUP PLAYLIST #2
Songs of England

When it comes to 'official' England songs, the FA can get it spectacularly right (see below, *World in Motion*), or calamitously wrong (see below, *We're On The Ball* by Ant 'n' also Dec). It is tempting to suppose that when they get it right it is by a happy accident, since the FA's idea of what England fans want, musically speaking, is betrayed by their insistence on 'officially' adopting that execrable brass band with their interminable looping of the theme from *The Great Escape*. Nonetheless, here are some England songs you might want to consider adding to your playlist...

⬤ ⬤ ⬤ ⬤ ⬤ *Three Lions (Football's Coming Home)* – Baddiel and Skinner and The Lightning Seeds

Not strictly speaking a World Cup song, fashioned as it was to accompany and celebrate the Euro 96 championships in England. Indeed, one of the most oddly touching images of that heart-breaking tournament was a shot of the two football-loving-but-not-especially-musical comics hearing their smash hit anthem being enthusiastically bellowed by a packed Wembley crowd.

Unfortunately, as we all know, football ultimately didn't come home in 1996, it pretty emphatically 'ging nach Hause' instead. The song did, however, climb back to the top of the charts in 1998 when the next World Cup was on, so it counts. Of course they had to change the words a bit. The years of hurt needed updating for a start (still counting), and they changed the title to Three Lions '98.

⦿ ⦿ ⦿ *Back Home* – 1970 England World Cup squad

In many ways the high water mark of that particular genre of football song – the type where footballers stand in a line in matching pullovers and mumble along unconvincingly to a jaunty little piece of jingoistic pop pap, their eyes trying to avoid the camera, but flicking to it self-consciously at regular intervals like a nervous tic.

In later years England fans simply wouldn't stand for this any more, but the 1970 World Cup squad contained so many players who had won the trophy four years earlier – Bobby Moore, Bobby Charlton, Gordon Banks, Alan Ball, Geoff Hurst, Martin Peters, Jack Charlton – that it seemed almost sacrilegious to suggest that they weren't going to retain the old Jules Rimet bauble.

It was Jeff Astle's atrocious vocal contribution on this that led to his twilit showbiz career singing live (and not significantly better) over the closing titles of Fantasy Football League. If only he'd notched that really easy chance in the group game against Brazil all would have been forgiven. Actually, it pretty much was forgiven – he seemed like a nice bloke, he could clearly take a joke, and it's not as if he made a pizza advert making light of England's penalty shoot-out debacles or anything. I mean, what kind of a man would do something like that...?

● ● *This Time (We'll Get it Right) / Fly The Flag*
– 1982 England World Cup squad

If *Back Home* was the finest hour of the uncomfortable and self-conscious team line up song, then this was surely its last hurrah. After this there was *We've Got The Whole World at our Feet* in 1986, which charted for one week only, and 1988's *All The Way*, which fared little better, before the whole world of the football song reinvented itself, all the way, forever.

The England squad's 1982 release was a double-A side. Frankly, the less said about *Fly The Flag* the better. *This Time (We'll Get It Right)*, however, is rather a jolly piece, written by a couple of lads with previous. Chris Norman and Pete Spencer of Smokie had written *Head Over Heels in Love* for Hamburg-based euro-pop sensation Kevin Keegan, and if only Keegan himself had been properly fit (for the tournament, that is, he was front-and-centre for the single) then maybe Ron's 22 would have got it right.

● ● ● ● ● *World in Motion* – New Order

From Kenneth Wolstenholme's revisiting of his classic "They think it's all over... it is now!" moment, through to John Barnes's somehow-not-naff rap – "There's only one way to beat them, get round the back" – this is far and away the most memorable, impressive and downright cool England song ever. The chances of that statement not still being true after the Gary Barlow / Gary Lineker / Gary Mabbutt offering rumoured to be on the way this year are nil.

The song was produced for England's Italia 90 campaign, and featured a number of team members. The ones credited are Peter Beardsley, Steve McMahon, Des Walker, John Barnes (of course) and also Geordie scamps Paul Gascoigne and Chris Waddle. The rest of the squad feature in the video miming along to the chorus and shouting "Express yourself!"

Also on show is comic Keith Allen, who wrote the words and got into the video, before going on to prove that lightning doesn't strike twice by bringing out the much less cool *Vindaloo* some years later with Fat Les.

Thankfully plans to re-release the song for the 2002 World Cup with a new rap done by David Beckham were shelved. What would that have been like?

"You've got to mo-del pants, and then get a tattoo, and before the première take the kids to the zoo..."

⚽ We're on the Ball – Ant 'n' Dec

Here's one you don't hear much nowadays. The Official England song for the 2002 World Cup was brought to a disbelieving public by those lads who used to be on Byker Grove and who ended up on Top of the Pops.

It was a retread of an old football song by a bloke who wrote *Nice One Cyril* and had a couple of pops at Eurovision in the seventies, most notably with Olivia Newton-John's song *Long Live Love*. Quite a pedigree, then.

It was thought that Ant 'n' Dec's profile as presenters of ITV's mediocrity sieve Pop Idol would help this malodorous item to the top of the pop parade, but actually it only made it to number 3, beaten by debut singles from

Will Young and Gareth Gates, who were the winner and runner-up respectively of the same series.

In the video the duo are seen wishing they could go to the World Cup, but thwarted because it is too expensive. So they go in disguise. They clearly think we are all idiots.

❸ *Diamond Lights – Glenn and Chris*

Not a World Cup song, or an England song, but a pop record released by two England World Cup stars in 1987. This is fondly remembered really for the performance of the two lads on Top of the Pops, jacket sleeves rolled up (as was the fashion at the time), Glenn Hoddle looking like he thought he was Lionel Richie, Chris Waddle looking like he thought it was all a terrible mistake. Waddle has said it was the most nerve-wracking thing he has ever done, which is saying something when you consider he once had to score a penalty to keep England in the World Cup semi-final, and almost booted the ball out of the ground. When he was interviewed for the England manager's job Hoddle was apparently asked: "Any skeletons in the closet... apart from that record with Chris Waddle?"

⦿ ⦿ ⦿ *World Cup Willie – Lonnie Donegan*

This is a novelty single from 1966, and possibly the only song dedicated to a World Cup mascot. World Cup Willie was "brave as a lion", according to the song, possibly because he was one. His image was on everything in the build up to the World Cup – beermats, badges, mugs, tankards, shirts, flags, cuddly toys, you name it – with his smiling face (lions are notoriously humorous) and his Union Jack shirt, as if to taunt the Scots, Welsh and Irish with their absence. I liked him.

Performed by Lonnie Donegan, the King of Skiffle, this jaunty little ditty in his honour delighted schoolchildren of all ages with its chorus of "Will-ieee! Will-ieee!"

WORLD CUP COLLECTABLES

Serbia Luxor

The advent of eBay means you no longer have to pester your Dad to go and fill the car up just so you can complete your World Cup coin collection. The internet also opens the door to wild and wonderful World Cup memorabilia from abroad.

For example, in 2006 there was a sticker collection in Serbia, where they were getting tremendously excited by the qualification of Serbia and Montenegro for the finals tournament in Germany.

Freed from the ghastly reverence accorded to footballers in this country under the baleful gaze of the Premier League and sundry image rights deals, well, they went for it big style.

Wayne Rooney, for example, is depicted as Shrek. We were all thinking it, obviously, but the Serbs went and actually did it.

Fernando Torres is shown as a baby (which we weren't all thinking, but they did it anyway).

Steven Gerrard, foxing them by having two first names, is shown with fire coming out of the ball, possibly as a result of an abortive attempt to serve up his favourite cheese (melted).

Nemanja Vidic, the home favourite, gets a double sticker in which he is shown as the hero of The Matrix – why not, why not indeed?

THREE LIONS

WAYNE ROONEY

NEMANJA VIDIC

ALBICELESTES

TEVEZ

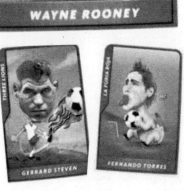

THREE LIONS

GERRARD STEVEN

LA FURIA ROJA

FERNANDO TORRES

Unfortunately for Neo-manja and his boys, the trip to Germany was a traumatic one. They got thumped 6-0 in the group stages by an Argentina side possibly inspired by the image of Carlos Tevez as a caveman, which would have taken care of the team talk.

HOW TO ENJOY THE WORLD CUP

IF YOU ARE... *an Astronaut*

In this era of low inter-galactic ambition, if you are an astronaut in space you are most likely orbiting in the International Space Station, and probably getting reasonable television coverage via the internet. These days it's not all eating food that looks like toothpaste and pooping in a funnel, you know.

Your companions are likely to be Russian or American (mainly interested in Groups G and H) or Chinese (mainly interested in telling you to get on with your experiments to see if ants can sort tiny screws in space).

Zero gravity is going to help with enjoying certain aspects of World Cup fun – recreating the Scorpion kick, for instance (see p.44), where it will dramatically reduce the dangers of hitting your chin on the floor. You will have the ability to perform goal celebrations that we mere mortals can only dream of – spinning cartwheels and toptails that will only stop when your esteemed international space colleagues grab you by the ankle and tell you to grow up.

Up in space nobody can hear you scream (unless you leave the microphone on), so it is also an excellent place to watch an England penalty shoot-out.

And you will have the opportunity, afforded to very few, of being able to see both participating countries in any given match out of your window *at the same time*. Iran v Argentina is going to be tough, admittedly – you might have to settle for alternating during that one...

WORLD CUP SKILLS #4

The Cruyff Turn

Johan Cruyff was already acclaimed as the best player in the world before the 1974 World Cup. Total Football was taking the world by storm, and Cruyff was its poster boy, the great individual player excelling in a new tactical style that was all about teamwork. He had won the Ballon d'Or three times, taken Ajax Amsterdam to three European Cups, and landed himself a big money transfer to Barcelona.

The single move that removed any lingering doubts was unveiled in the second group game of that World Cup, against Sweden. The Dutch master received a long ball in the left wing position, outside the area, then turned to face the Swedish full back, Jan Olsson. Cruyff drifted away from the goal, looking up, for all the world as though he was about to dink the ball into the penalty area with his right foot. Instead, he suddenly twisted, dragging the ball with his right foot behind his planted left foot, and darted towards the goal line to cross it with his left.

Olsson bought the dummy as surely as if Cruyff had pointed towards the centre circle and said "Look, isn't that Agnetha out of Abba in a really short skirt...?", almost tumbling to the floor in bewilderment when he realised Cruyff had gone.

183

Previously in Brazil

The FIFA World Cup has been to Brazil before, in 1950. What follows is a story from then...

The four British football associations of England, Scotland, Wales and Northern Ireland had withdrawn from FIFA in 1920. There were disagreements over the advisability of playing matches against countries with whom Britain had so recently been at war, and this isolationist policy meant that there was no home participation in any of the first three World Cups.

In the aftermath of the Second World War FIFA was desperate to bring the British teams back into the international fold, particularly to give legitimacy to their ailing revival of the World Cup in 1950. They offered the British associations a vice-presidency, and a guaranteed place on FIFA's executive committee.

In addition, FIFA offered the winners of the 1950 Home Internationals a place in the World Cup finals, thus guaranteeing that there would be a British team at the tournament. This was an extremely, even controversially, generous gesture, considering that everyone else was having to play tricky home and away qualifiers. The Brits still weren't convinced, though, and so FIFA offered to invite the runners-up as well, meaning two of the four British sides were guaranteed a place in Brazil.

Incredibly, George Graham (not that one), secretary of the Scottish Football Association, said that Scotland would only send a team if they were the British champions, they wouldn't go as runners up.

In 1950 there was no Scotland manager. The team was chosen by an international selection committee, which made some curious decisions. The Scots began with an 8-2 thrashing of Northern Ireland, in which Henry Morris of East Fife scored a debut hat trick. He never played for Scotland again. Then Scotland beat Wales 2-0, with Clyde's Alec Linwood notching the second on his debut. He never played for Scotland again either.

Meanwhile England also beat Northern Ireland (9-2) and Wales (4-1). Second place at least was thus guaranteed. For the crucial decider against England, Scotland lined up with three more debutants (including one that some of the selectors had never seen play), knowing that a draw would mean they were joint champions, and could accept FIFA's invitation with their heads held high.

It was not to be. England won 1-0 through a Roy Bentley goal. Scotland's captain George Young, pleaded with the SFA's executive committee to back down and send the team to Brazil, but Graham refused, saying that Scotland had given their word and that was that.

Was it arrogance? Pig-headedness? Or just that they couldn't afford the expense? Some of the selections did seem unnecessarily risky, almost like they were trying to miss out. But what would Scotland not have given for a soft qualification like that in 2014...?

FOOD AND DRINK

Caipirinha

Now, if you really want to get into the spirit of the Brazil World Cup – and by spirit, I mean, you know, *spirit* – then you should get yourself a bottle of cachaça. Cachaça is a distilled spirit made from sugar cane, and is the most popular spirit in Brazil. In fact it is so popular that Brazilians have almost as many names for the stuff as Eskimos do for snow. Some of these names are affectionate nicknames, others were coined to sidestep the authorities during the days when cachaça was actually banned in Brazil. So it is called, among many other things, *aguardente*, *pinga*, *caninha*, *abre-coraçao* (heart-opener), *água-benta* (holy water), *bafo-de-tigre* (tiger breath), and *limpa-olho* (eye-wash).

Cachaça can be drunk straight – of course it can, it's a liquid. Its most popular role, however, is as the chief ingredient of the *caipirinha*, the national cocktail.

I reckon we're going to hear a lot about these caipirinhas during the World Cup, especially in arch broadcaster sign-offs – "That's all from me, I'm off to enjoy a swift *caipirinha* down the Copacabana...!" – designed to make people back home feel jealous of the cushy gig they have landed. Gary Lineker is definitely going to mention them.

HOW TO MAKE A CAIPIRINHA:

Take an old-fashioned glass, one of those stubby ones with a heavy bottom. Put in half a lime cut into four wedges and two teaspoonfuls of brown sugar. The lime is to counteract the too-sweet sugarcane spirit, and the sugar to counteract the tartness of the lime.

Then take your muddler (what do you mean, you haven't got a muddler? Do you know what a muddler is? It's a sort of wooden bartender's tool, like a pestle, used to mash ingredients together to release their flavour. Well, use a wooden spoon if you must...) and mash the lime segments and sugar together. Then fill the glass with crushed ice and add the cachaça.

That's all there is to it. You don't have to shake it, and you don't have to stir it, never mind choose between the two, which is probably why James Bond never bothers with them.

Drink too many, the saying goes, and you'll be seeing pink dolphins walking on the beach.

THE WATCHING AN ENGLAND GAME
DRINKING GAME

> ! REMEMBER: ALWAYS WATCH ENGLAND GAMES IN MODERATION, AND DON'T TRY TO DRIVE OR OPERATE HEAVY MACHINERY AFTERWARDS. i

THE RULES

Watch the camera pan along the lines of players during the National Anthems. If the number of players who clearly don't know the words exceeds the number of players confidently singing along – have yourself a pre-match snifter.

The game kicks off. Have a drink – the scores are level, and we're still in it!

An England full back has the ball in a good crossing position. He boots the ball high over the area, at least ten feet over the head of England's tallest striker, and it goes straight out for a goal kick. Have a drink, and put 50p in the swear tin.

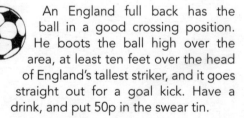

England score a goal! We're going to win the Cup! Have a celebratory drink!

 Referee books someone. If it is an opposition player have a drink. If it's an England player have a drink, and put 50p in the swear tin.

  England concede a goal! We're going home! Have a consolatory drink!

 There is a stoppage of some kind, and all the England players run to the touchline to get themselves a drink in the hot and humid conditions. Man, it looks hot out there. They look really thirsty... Better have a drink to join in.

 In the crowd you catch a glimpse of a bunch of WAGs (wives or girlfriends – it's a flawed acronym). Have a drink in their honour.

 Half time. Depending on how the first half has gone you may well need a comfort break, and then you might want to get a bit of pizza or some sandwiches, just in case you need to soak up more punishment in the second half.

If the game is on ITV, then each of you should guess the odds that the giant floating head of Ray Winstone is going to offer you the chance to "'ave a bang on". Nearest wins, everyone else drains their glass.

The ball hits the frame of the goal, the post or the bar. Everyone shouts out (US soccerball style) "POLE SHOT!" Last one to do so empties their glass.

Joe Hart mishandles. Have a drink. If the Brazuca ball is blamed, make it a *caipirinha*.

A possession stat flashes up on the screen, and England have had the lion's share of the ball. Have a drink. If England have hardly had any of the ball, have two drinks.

In the crowd you spot Sepp Blatter. At an England game? Surely he's made some kind of mistake? Have a quick drink, otherwise the drinks you've already had may find their way back up...

Referee sends someone off. If an opposition player, do a prematurely triumphal jig, and have a drink. If an England player, have a drink and put 50p in the swear tin. If the offence is a petulant bit of retaliation, have two drinks, then begin work on an effigy of the player concerned (see p.208).

Roy Hodgson brings on a sub. Have a drink. If it is Tom Cleverley have a big drink – you'll need it.

PHEEEEP! Final whistle. England have **WON**! Have a drink to celebrate.

PHEEEEP! Final whistle. England have **LOST**! Have two drinks to take the edge off.

 PHEEEEP! Final whistle. England have **DRAWN**. Have a drink to calm down, unless it is a knockout game and we are going into extra time, in which case don't have a drink – you need to pace yourself.

The game ends level after extra time, and there will be a penalty shootout. Have five drinks before it starts, and with a bit of luck you'll miss the whole thing and can read about it in the paper in two or three days' time.

BRAZIL IN FACTS #3

The Mighty Amazon

The Amazon is the greatest river in the world by so many measures. It is fed by the largest drainage basin in the world, covering approximately 40 percent of South America. Its water flow exceeds the next seven largest rivers in the world combined, and represents one fifth of all the freshwater discharged into the world's oceans. During the dry season the river can be six miles wide, but when it gets wet it floods to 25 miles, and the mouth is 200 miles across. The rainforests of the Amazon basin are home to millions of species of plants and animals, including piranha, anaconda, electric eels, stingray and even sharks.

In fact, the Amazon holds so many records that it must be galling for Amazon fans to have to acknowledge that the Nile is actually the longest river in the world. Indeed, in 2007 a group of Brazilian scientists announced new calculations that "proved" the Amazon was longer – when measured from its source in the Andes to the tidal estuary, and then round some suspiciously unnecessary-looking loops to include the marine waters of the Rio Para bay. (In fairness they then used the same method to recalculate the Nile's length and found it was also longer than previously thought, but still not as long as the Amazon.)

The Amazon takes its name from an incident in which 16th-century Spanish explorer Francisco de Orellana and his men were attacked by fierce female warriors, who beat many of them to death with clubs. The Spaniards likened these women to the Amazons of Greek mythology, and the name Rio de Amazonas stuck.

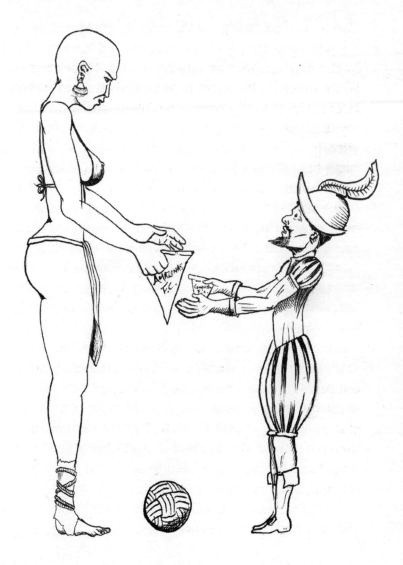

WORLD CUP PLAYLIST #3

Songs of Other Lands, Other World Cups

After the draw was concluded, FIFA announced that there would be a contest to discover the "official" World Cup song for 2014, a process that would be overseen by Ricky Martin. Frankly, I think we'd all be happier with Ricky Lambert in charge of things, but there we are.

In the end they announced that they were going with a collaboration between noted chart-topping rapper Pitbull (Cuban-American) and Jennifer Lopez (American-American), with a token (far from it, what are you talking about?) contribution from Brazilian singer Claudia Leitte. The song was called *We Are One (Ole Ola)*.

Pitbull – who may have come to FIFA's attention by trademarking his nickname, Mr Worldwide, before Sepp Blatter could get round to it – may do the business. Who knows? Here, in advance of that, are some songs from other lands, and other World Cups, you might want to consider for your playlist...

⚫⚫⚫ *Waka Waka (This Time For Africa)* – The Official 2010 World Cup Song, by Shakira featuring Freshlyground

If I'd asked you to guess what was the most successful World Cup song ever, would you have guessed this one? Well, it is one of the most colossal hits of all time. All time, in football terms, means "since the start of the Premiership", of course, but this tops songs that are even older than that. Pre-time itself. It is something like the seventh most watched vid on youtube. 570,000 hits it has had, and no one falls off anything or gets a pet to play a musical instrument. Mind you, Shakira is wearing a very short skirt. Very short indeed.

There was a fair amount of controversy over FIFA's choice of Shakira, a Colombian artiste, for their "official" 2010 World Cup song, given the wealth of African (and particularly South African) musical talent available, which might have been more appropriate given the venue of the tournament. However, Shakira won World Cup music lovers over by teaming up with African musos Freshlyground. And it is a very catchy little number.

For myself, I was just disappointed that the title does not seem to be a referential tribute to the catchphrase of Fozzie Bear off of *The Muppets* ("The comedian's a bear!" "No he's not, he's a-wearing a neck-a-tie!")

●●●●● *Nessun Dorma* – Luciano Pavarotti

This is one of the great show-off arias of opera, and it comes from Puccini's *Turandot*. At first glance the storyline doesn't seem to have much in common with the world of top class international sport. Prince Calàf, who is singing the aria, has fallen for the heartless Princess Turandot. She has so far avoided marriage thanks to one of those fairytale gimmicks whereby she gets to ask any prospective suitor three riddles, and if he can't answer them she can kill him.

When Calàf, our hero, passes the test, Turandot throws such an unattractive paddy that he gives her another chance to wriggle out of marrying him. If she can discover his name – he has so far competed anonymously – by dawn he will submit to death. It's really a sort of upmarket all-or-nothing snuff version of *Rumpelstiltskin*. So when he is singing *nessun dorma*, none shall sleep, he means that he is not going to be nodding off any time soon because of worrying about the bizarre situation, and no one else will sleep because they are trying to find out his name to get the cruel Princess T off the hook. Or else she'll kill all of them instead. That's what she's like – she's quite a catch.

Where the aria connects with football is that it is shot through with edge-of-the-seat nail-biting anxiety about something you don't know the result of and cannot influence. The final rousing climactic lines, when the dawn arrives and Calàf comes to believe that victory is within his grasp – *Vincero!* I shall win! – could hardly be more aptly applicable to the emotional state of a football fan whose team is a goal up in injury time, and he's daring to dream of a semi-final against a slightly weaker team whose best player is suspended.

Luciano Pavarotti's performance was the theme for the BBC's World Cup coverage in 1990. Its soaring emotional mix of fear and hope brings a lump to the throat still, dissolving in the mind's eye to a mental image of Desmond Lynam with his fingers crossed.

However, it wasn't just in our country that *Nessun Dorma* was inextricably linked to Italia 90. The international phenomenon that was The Three Tenors (Pavarotti, Plácido Domingo and José Carreras, who I always think of as "the other one" because of that *Seinfeld* episode) made its debut concert on the eve of the final at the Baths of Caracalla in Rome, and they reinforced their World Cup credentials by cropping up again in Los Angeles in 1994, at the Eiffel Tower in 1998 and at Yokohama in 2002.

●●●● *Pam Pam Cameroon* – Macka B

Unusually for a World Cup song this came out post- tournament as a celebration of Cameroon's glorious exploits at Italia 90 where they became the first African team to make it to the quarter finals. It is a catchy little reggae number, and some of the lyrics are just hilarious.

It begins with the singer, Macka B, thinking back to Cameroon's World Cup and chuckling "Makanaky! Heh heh heh..!" to himself. Then he takes us through the Roger Milla-inspired victories over Argentina and Romania, which meant that Cameroon were surprise early qualifiers for the knockout stages so that when they played

Russia in their final group match "they lose four-nil but it never mattah!"

Leave it to Macka B to describe what happened next as crisply and clearly as an action replay:

The next team they play was Colombia,
and them they have a fool fool goalkeepah,
See him try to dribble past Roger Milla,
see Milla a-laugh as he score de winnah!

The real triumph, however, comes when we get to the verse about Cameroon's extra time quarter final defeat to England, courtesy of two Gary Lineker penalties. Not for Macka B the sporting shrug or the wistful so-near-yet-so far. No, he plugs into that most deeply rooted of football fan certainties – that defeat tastes most bitter when you are sure your team was superior and have been shafted. Here's how the verse goes:

They were lucky lucky, very lucky lucky,
Against the Cameroon England were lucky lucky
They were lucky lucky, very lucky lucky,
Against the Cameroon England were lucky lucky.
It was luck.

He follows this with a little jovial racism about how black people are better than white people, all to a jaunty reggae beat – and you'll be singing its catchy hook for days.

⬤⬤ *Gloryland* – Daryl Hall and Sounds of Blackness

This was performed at the opening ceremony of USA 94 – you know, the one where Diana Ross missed an open goal – and was also used as the theme to ITV's coverage of the tournament. It is essentially *Glory, Glory, Hallelujah*, but with Daryl Hall bombastically doing his own thing in front of a gospel choir. Actually, it's lucky they're there, because it's quite hard to recognise the tune from what Daryl is doing. The words, specially written for the World Cup – "it's in your heart, it's in your hands" – betray the Americans' poor grasp of the rules of the game. You may find it rousing. I find it a bit much.

⬤⬤⬤⬤ *Wavin' Flag* – K'naan

This uplifting anthem became associated with the 2010 World Cup when it was used by Coca-Cola (one of the Official Partners of the FIFA 2010 World Cup™) in an advertising campaign. Despite this it was adopted by football fans around the world during the tournament, who, after all, like nothing more than waving flags.

The song has an interesting history. Originally, the Somalian-Canadian singer K'naan wrote the song about the struggles of refugees displaced by war, and the aspirations of the people of Somalia for freedom. It was re-recorded and released as a charity single by a Canadian Band Aid-style supergroup after the Haiti earthquake of 2010. The later version released for the World Cup had different, more celebratory, lyrics, all about rejoicing in the beautiful game, and the nations of the world singing under the setting sun, but somehow it retains some of the hope and belief in the human spirit of the original as well. So why not wave the flag?

●●● *El Rock del Mundial – Los Ramblers*

This is an upbeat rockabilly anthem from the 1962 World Cup, performed by Chilean group Los Ramblers, who, incredibly, are still going more than half a century on. They're like Status Quo, or The Shadows. Presumably they spend most of their time nowadays making talking head contributions to rockumentaries about people they once knew who are now dead.

The song, with its route one title ("World Cup Rock"), is straight down the middle, chested down by the big centre forward and smashed home. As you listen to it you can almost see girls in big dresses being swung around by blokes in leather jackets in American-style diners. What that's got to do with the World Cup? Who knows?

●●●● *The Cup of Life* – Ricky Martin

The year before *Livin' la Vida Loca*, Ricky Martin burst onto the international scene with this anthem for the 1998 World Cup. His performance of *La Copa de la Vida* at the Grammy Awards is widely credited with kick-starting the Latin pop explosion, opening the door for artists such as Jennifer Lopez, Enrique Iglesias and Shakira. Although it didn't do much business in the UK, it topped charts almost everywhere else and was a big breakthrough hit for the lad.

The lyrics, in English and Spanish, aren't up to much, from the football fan's perspective. "Do you really want it? Go go go! Here we go! Push it along, right to the top!" – he could be talking about anything (ahem...). But it is a high-energy performance, and if you like this sort of thing it's a good 'un.

HOW TO ENJOY THE WORLD CUP

IF YOU ARE... *a Politician*

History is littered with examples of politicians who have fallen foul of trying to suck up to sports fans. Tony Blair, for instance, proved no more adept at taking penalties than Diana Ross, and looked a complete twit trying to do headed keepy-uppies with Kevin Keegan. Boris Johnson managed to make the Olympic velodrome look dull merely by cycling round it, and got stuck on a zip wire above the Olympic park while celebrating Team GB's first gold medal. So don't do that.

Harold Wilson was fond of pointing out that England only ever won the World Cup under a Labour government (as true today as it has ever been) and confidently called a General Election during the 1970 World Cup in Mexico expecting to cash in on a rousing run to the semis, not reckoning on Gordon Banks's tummy bug and Peter Bonetti's big match nerves bringing us Edward Heath in Number 10, the three-day week, and ultimately Thatcherism.

Our current esteemed Coalition leader has a terrible record of jinxing British sports stars, so we might all enjoy it more if he just does us all a favour and shuts up for a month. Maybe Dave might enjoy choosing what nibbles to offer Roy and the boys when he invites them over to bask in their reflected glory once it is all over and the open-top bus pulls into Downing Street.

There's no denying that the World Cup is going to take up a disproportionate amount of the News Cycle, so if you are Ian Duncan Smith, say, it might be a good time to sneak out another announcement of some mean-spirited benefit cut you don't want people to notice...

QUIZ #3

Q1: Which World Cup final took place in the Stadium of the National Fascist Party?

Q2: Which two Wimbledon players featured in Jamaica's squad at the 1998 World Cup?

Q3: What is the name of the technique Ronaldinho claimed to have used when he fluked his free kick over David Seaman's pony-tailed head in the 2002 quarter final in Shizuoka?

Q4: Who scored the clinching penalty in the Republic of Ireland's second round shootout with Romania at Italia 90?

Q5: Which member of England's 2010 World Cup squad was playing his club football for a team that are now to be found in League Division 2?

Q6: What nationality was the player booked three times in a match by Graham Poll?

Q7: Which three teams has Guus Hiddink managed at the World Cup finals?

Q8: Which five Arsenal players were in France's 2010 World Cup squad?

Q9: Which was the first African country to progress beyond the first group stage of a World Cup finals?

Q10: Who were the goalscorers in the 1970 World Cup final?

Q11: The first World Cup mascot was World Cup Willie in 1966. Can you name any three of the ones designed for subsequent tournaments? Go on, have a go. Any three...

Q12: Who scored Scotland's goal against Iran in Córdoba in 1978?

Q13: Which team has been knocked out at the quarter-final stage most often?

Q14: When was the first time a European nation beat a South American nation in a World Cup final

Q15: In 1986 at Nezahualcóyotl José Batista was sent off in the first minute of a group game for a foul on Gordon Strachan – who did Batista play for?

Q16: Why did Perugia's president, Luciano Gaucci, tell his club's star forward that he was fired during the 2002 World Cup?

Q17: Which two Arsenal players were selected for Esso's Italia 90 England coin squad, but not the actual squad?

Q18: What was the name of the Italian left back who broke German hearts with his 119th minute goal in the semi-final in 2006, and then scored the clinching penalty in the shootout after extra time at the final.

Q19: Patrice Evra blamed the sound of the long plastic horns that fans played at the 2010 World Cup for France's poor performance – but what were the horns called?

Q20: Ronaldinho made his debut for Gremio as an 18 year-old in 1998, and didn't make his international debut until a year later. So how come Ronaldinho won a bronze medal at the 1996 Olympic tournament?

Answers on p.223

WORLD CUP SKILLS #5

The Rabona

The Rabona is not associated with any particular World Cup. It is, however, South American in origin, and there are so many potential demonstrators at the tournament this time (Balotelli, Ronaldo, Hazard, Villa, Sneijder, Nani and van der Vaart have all done it in big games) that it is almost bound to come up.

Usually (but not always) the Rabona is performed by a right-footed player attacking down the left. Instead of using his left foot to cross, he swings his right leg behind his left and crosses the ball with his right foot.

This will elicit one of three responses: 1. "Wow!" 2. "Why didn't he cross it with his left foot?" And 3. (when attempted by David Dunn of Blackburn Rovers) "Look at that silly bugger flat on his face, what did he think he was doing?"

The Rabona was supposedly first performed in an Argentinian club game by Ricardo Infante in 1948, leading to a punning headline which translates as 'Infante Played Hooky' (*rabona* means skipping school in Spanish).

The first filmed Rabona was pulled off by Pelé in 1957, and it is the only football move to have been turned into a dance step in the tango.

NB: If you try this in your garden and dislocate your knee I take no responsibility.

207

HARNESS THE POWER OF
VOODOO-TTEO

Superstition is a massive part of football, both for players and supporters.

There are players who feel they have to put their left boot on first, or (I'm looking at you, Johann Cruyff) to slap their goalkeeper in the stomach just before kick-off.

For supporters it could be wearing a pair of lucky pants, or eating a special pre-match lunch, or avoiding the cracks in the pavement on the way to the game.

If you want to take things a step further you could try Voodoo-teo. Yes, you heard me.

The day after England were knocked out of the World cup in 2002 I was wandering aimlessly around Osaka, and bought a bottle of a popular aerated beverage, that also happened to be an Official Partner of the FIFA 2002 World Cup™. There was a free gift attached, which turned out to be a little plastic model of Rivaldo, the least sporting of the Three Rs, to whom I had taken a particular dislike only the afternoon before. As it happens I found myself at the top of an ancient cobbled street called Nannen-zaka; legend has it that if you stumble while walking down it you will only have bad luck thereafter.

"Right," I said to myself, and bounced the little plastic Rivaldo over the cobbles, booting him down to the bottom, and sure enough he hardly had a kick for the rest of the tournament.

Unfortunately I had discovered the power of Voodoo-tteo 24 hours too late to help Sven, Becks and the lads on that occasion. But if enough of us are prepared to put in the time and effort maybe we can make a difference this time (more than any other time).

What you need to do is get hold of some plastic Subbutteo figures. Maybe you have some old ones you'd be prepared to sacrifice. Maybe you'll need to go out and get some new ones. Ask yourself this: how much do you really *want* it?

Then you need to pick the opposition player from an upcoming match most likely to make the difference. Then you paint a Subbutteo figure until it looks as much like the player in question as possible – get the kit exactly right, paint the shirt number and name on the back, check for any other details, such as beards, moustaches, birth marks (amazing what you can find on Google™).

Or you can just leave one up against the radiator for a bit and it will end up looking like Bastian Schweinsteiger.

Then, when you are satisfied with your handiwork, take your little figure out into the garden and stamp it to bits. Might work – you never know.

FOOD AND DRINK
Guaraná Antarctica

If you are making a serious attempt to get your kids interested in the World Cup, then you may feel an obligation to ease off the *caipirinhas* when they are around.

But never fear – there is a massively popular Brazilian soft drink too. It's called Guaraná Antarctica, and it is the second best-selling soft drink brand in Brazil after Coca-Cola. Ironically, given the sickly sweetness of both products, their rivalry is a bitter one.

The guaraná is a climbing plant of the maple family which produces a caffeine-rich fruit the size of a coffee bean. The flavour is like apple and berry, apparently.

Guaraná Antarctica are the official sponsor of the Brazilian national football team. Coca-Cola, of course, are official partners of the FIFA World Cup, so we could be in store for some entertaining soft-drink-related fireworks. Remember in 2010 when a certain Dutch brewery got tickets for 30 gorgeous girls dressed in orange miniskirts as a piece of so-called 'guerrilla' marketing for their beer? And FIFA had them all arrested because they weren't representing the official brewers of the FIFA World Cup? Well, if you see a bloke in a penguin costume with guaraná berries round his neck being hustled to the exit by Sepp Blatter's bully boys then you'll know what is occurring.

Four years and one World Cup earlier, Guaraná

Antarctica ran a series of commercials featuring Argentine handball legend Diego Maradona. He was featured wearing the yellow jersey of Brazil and singing the Brazilian national anthem, before waking up and declaring that it was a nightmare brought on by too much guaraná the night before. This caused considerable controversy in Argentina, but Maradona wasn't bothered. He just used the Hand of God to shove the Wallet of God into the Back Pocket of God and went on his merry butterball way.

It is difficult to see how the Maradona advert was supposed to work. Guaraná Antarctica gives you nightmares – was that the message? And nobody in Brazil is going to buy something because Maradona likes it. It is a bit like if Fanta claimed that Fanta was short for 'Fantastisch!" and it was invented by Hitler.

HIT THE HEADLINES

Now surely – surely – BRAZIL NUTS! is going to feature as a tabloid headline at some point during the World Cup. The tabloid boys love a foodstuff, especially one they can photoshop somebody's face onto, like they did with poor old Graham 'Turnip' Taylor back at Euro 1992. Frankly, SWEDES 2 TURNIPS 1 is the high water mark they've been struggling to reach ever since.

But what will the story be?

It could be a crazy sending off, in the mould of Roo in 2006 or Becks in 1998.

It could be an unfathomable selection howler, such as Roy putting Andy Carroll on the left wing (or even in the squad at all).

Or will they hold fire until they get a good old fashioned ball-in-the-bollocks impact, such as happened to Rivaldo in 2002, when he fell to the floor clutching his face as though he'd been punched?

Who knows?

HOW TO ENJOY THE WORLD CUP

IF YOU ARE... *Scottish*

You could support England, have you thought of that? We supported Andy Murray, and he doesn't make it easy. And look at all the fuss we were able to make over him as a result. We supported Ally McLeod's drug-addled Tartan Army last time there was a South American World Cup back in 1978, right up to the so-near-yet-so-far brinkmanship of that Archie Gemmill-inspired comeback against Holland.

You too could have some of that vicarious enjoyment if England won a game or two. But oh no, it's got to be ABE - Anyone But England. Have you thought about how that makes us feel? Especially those of us with my particular surname? No, of course you haven't. You still want England to lose against whoever they are playing, even if it's the Germans. Whatever happened to that Dunkirk spirit, all in it together against the Hun? Or what about the Falklands-coveting Argies? Surely there's room in your hearts to support England if we play them? No? Well then I don't care if you enjoy the World Cup. There, I've said it...

Previously in Brazil

The FIFA World Cup has been to Brazil before, in 1950. What follows is a story from then...

This was England's first appearance at a World Cup, and there were certainly grounds for confidence. England were a force at international level, and their forwards – Finney, Mortensen, Milburn, Bentley and Mannion – had been scoring goals for fun.

Stanley Matthews had had a great season for Blackpool, but he had been left out despite a public clamour for his recall. Instead he was sent with a 'B' team to Canada, where his performances were so impressive that the FA finally bowed to pressure and diverted him to Rio as a late addition to the squad.

The food in the hotel wasn't up to much. Alf Ramsey was the first to get ill, and it was the memory of this that prompted him to bring so much food from England to Mexico for the 1970 tournament. Before long the squad was subsisting mainly on bananas, and when Mortensen was asked if this was an ideal diet for football he said "No, but you should see us climbing trees!"

England found themselves in a group along with Chile, Spain and the United States. They began with an unconvincing 2-0 win over Chile, before heading to Belo Horizonte to play the United States. The Americans were mostly semi-professional players with other jobs. There was a high school teacher, a hearse driver, a dishwasher, and even the mandatory postman without which no plucky underdog outfit is truly complete. Three of their players were not actually US citizens. Ed McIlvenny (Scottish), Joe Maca (Belgian) and Joe Gaetjens (Haitian) had merely indicated their intention to apply for citizenship, which was enough for them to be selected.

They were 500-1 to win the cup, but had given a good account of themselves against Spain, leading 1-0 until fifteen minutes from time before losing 3-1. Nevertheless, before the England game their coach Bill Jeffrey (Scottish) told the press "We have no chance. They are sheep ready to be slaughtered".

England kicked off. Chances came thick and fast, but none were converted by England's stellar forward line, and in the 38th minute a long shot glanced into the net off the head of Joe Gaetjens to give the USA the lead.

The second half brought a prolonged onslaught from England, but the American part-timers held out for one of the biggest shocks in World Cup history. The Brazilian crowd went wild, hoping that this would mean their team would not have to play England later on, and so it proved, as England were beaten again in their last match against Spain.

Legend has it that the newspapers assumed the result coming down the wires was a mistake and printed a 10-1 England win, but this seems to be untrue – and in fact more headlines were made by the England cricket team losing for the first time to the West Indies.

The blue shirt with red numbers that England sported for this debâcle was never used again.

THE
BIG MATCH

ITV vs BBC

One enjoyable aspect of a World Cup is the way the two main national broadcasters go head to head. They don't actually cover the same matches, of course, until the final, but they are both covering the event as a whole, and so definitely in direct competition.

Let's start with the anchormen. **Gary Lineker** is a crisp operator (also a crisp salesman), and comes with the authority of 80 caps and 48 international goals. He is also England's top World Cup goalscorer (with his ten), and highly likely still to be so at the end of this tournament (if he isn't someone will have had a *whale* of a time).

Lineker's speciality is the leaden witty sign off. You know everything about it has been carefully weighed and measured beforehand, with just the right amount of cheekiness added to 41 percent punmanship, and a friendly self-deprecating dollop of Christmas cracker awfulness so that we'll still like him and won't think he's getting too big for his golden boots.

Adrian Chiles has followed a well-worn path from the BBC over to ITV (Desmond Lynam, Bob Wilson, Steve Rider, Sooty...), leaving at almost the very instant his favourite-cushion face had found a perfect home on the *One Show* sofa.

If Chiles hits you with a zinger, he's just thought of it – and more than likely hasn't thought it through. For instance, when he says a game is so tedious that he'll send a fiver to anyone who's still awake he hasn't quite worked out that he is talking to an audience, an ITV audience, who will drag him kicking and screaming through the fires of hell until he has actually paid them an actual fiver.

So Chiles is likely to give you the wilder ride, but both are capable pairs of hands.

What about the other guys around the shonkily-designed perspex tables?

The BBC's "presentation team" is to be Thierry Henry, Rio Ferdinand, Alan Shearer, Phil Neville, Alan Hansen, and Clarence Seedorf. The World Cup is the mighty Hansen's last hurrah, and the BBC have planned a great send off-for him by plonking him next to Rio Ferdinand, whose bluff has emphatically been called after he described *Match of the Day* as "too dull to watch" last year. What price Rio to be caught on Twitter during a half-time analysis? Perhaps tweeting about how dull Alan Shearer is?

Phil Neville has been hired seemingly on the basis that his brother is good at working the special screen gizmos on Sky. Thierry Henry and Clarence Seedorf are there to provide the sort of urbanity and wit that is normally the preserve of Robbie "Sav" Savage, so things could be worse. Much, *much* worse.

Chiles, meanwhile, will be chatting to Glenn Hoddle (on loan for internationals only from Sky), Lee Dixon, Roy Keane, Patrick Vieira and smiley Roberto Martinez.

ITV's press release hyped Hoddle as "the only living footballer to have played for and managed England at a World Cup", a somewhat tortuous construction that seems to imply that they would have got Alf Ramsey (who played all England's matches in 1950, and managed the England team with somewhat more success than Hoddle did) except he was dead, or Kevin

Keegan (who played in 1982 and managed England at a European Championships) except they didn't.

Lucky old Glenn, I say. He must have been a really good boy in a previous life to land a gig like this.

Roy Keane will be sitting there pundificating about the importance of the World Cup. though he's the only man to have given up the chance of competing in one because the training facilities weren't up to scratch. Of course, he might not be sitting there. If his hotel room hasn't got a minibar he'll be back in Cheshire walking his big dogs.

Lee Dixon may have interesting observations to make, as long as he's not distracted by that terrifying beardy half-smile of Keane's that makes him look like he wants to bite someone's arm off. Patrick Vieira is there to man-mark him, and also the Beeb's Thierry Henry, and Roberto Martinez looks like the kind of fellow who will enjoy himself wherever he is.

As for the commentary teams, they lack something of the gravitas of tournaments gone by, with the passing of David Coleman and Brian Moore, and the retirements of John Motson and Barry Davies (from live football anyway – Motty still does highlights, and Barry still does *The Jump*, Channel Four's celebrity ice-task-based train wreck). The battle will be taken up by two identikit gangs of charisma-free functionaries, from which you may be able to pick out the excitable yapping of Jonathan Pearce and the portentous overkill of Clive Tyldesley.

WORLD CUP QUIZ ANSWERS

WORLD CUP QUIZ #1

A1: Jamie Carragher missed the Slovenia group game in 2010 after picking up bookings in the first two matches.

A2: Mick Mills stood in for the injured Kevin Keegan, who only managed the last 27 minutes of England's last match.

A3: In those pre-shoot-out days, there would have been a flip of a coin to determine the World Champion. Doesn't bear thinking about, does it...?

A4: Dutch East Indies.

A5: Adidas.

A6: Mexico 1970

A7: Stuart Pearce, Chris Waddle, David Batty, Paul Ince, Frank Lampard, Steven Gerrard and Jamie Carragher

A8: *Don't Come Home Too Soon* by Del Amitri. A forlorn hope, really.

A9: Ferenc Puskas.

A10: Jerome Boateng (Germany) and Kevin Prince Boateng (Ghana)

A11: Pierluigi Collina.

A12: Trevor Brooking

A13: Because of the Anschluss, when their country was annexed by Germany. Actually several Austrian players joined the German squad. When Germany lost in the first round, coach Sepp Herberger blamed this on the defeatist attitude of the five Austrians he had been obliged to pick.

A14: In a shoebox under the bed of the Italian vice-president of FIFA, Dr Ottorino Barassi.

A15: It was in Detroit, at the Pontiac Silverdome Stadium, in 1994, between the USA and Switzerland.

A16: Roker Park in Sunderland, Ayresome Park in Middlesbrough, and White City in London.

A17: Gerry Hitchens (Inter Milan, 1962), Tony Woodcock (1.FC Köln, 1982), Ray Wilkins (AC Milan, 1986), Mark Hateley (AC Milan, 1986), Chris Waddle (Marseille, 1990), Owen Hargreaves (Bayern Munich, 2002, 2006) and David Beckham (Real Madrid, 2006).

A18: Manuel Neuer. Surely some kind of retrospective ban is in order?

A19: Ayrton Senna. The Formula One driver died two and a half months earlier.

A20: Stephen Warnock, James Milner and Emile Heskey.

WORLD CUP QUIZ # 2

A1: Tom Finney, v Soviet Union 1958 – 36 years 64 days.

A2: Ray Wilkins (1986), David Beckham (1998) and Wayne Rooney (2006)

A3: Black.

A4: Paul Gascoigne

A5: Because the two teams could not agree on which ball to use, so Argentina's ball was used for the first half (after which Argentina were 2-1 up) and then Uruguay's for the second half (during which Uruguay made the score 4-2 in their favour).

A6: Terry Butcher, Chris Woods, Gary Stevens, Trevor Steven (all Rangers, all 1990).

A7: Helmut Haller of West Germany. Geoff Hurst scored a hat trick, but it was Haller who nicked off with the match ball. It was finally tracked down by the Daily Mirror in 1996, who paid Haller £80,000 for it, and it now resides at the National Football Museum in Manchester.

A8: Tommy Wright.

A9: Joe Jordan in 1974 (v Yugoslavia and Zaire), 1978 (v Peru) and 1982 (v Soviet Union), and David Beckham in 1998 (v Colombia), 2002 (v Argentina) and 2006 (v Ecuador)

A10: José Luis Brown, Jorge Valdano, Jorge Burruchaga, Karl-Heinz Rummenigge and Rudi Völler

A11: Paul. Full name: Paul the Octopus.

A12: Placido Domingo, Henry Kissinger and Johan Cruyff (see chapter: Sepp Blatter gets something wrong). Massive kudos if you got any of these. I really only put this one in because it's funny.

A13: Mark Hateley

A14: Patrick Battiston

A15: Pedro Monzon and Gustavo Dezotti (Argentina) in 1990, Zinedine Zidane (France) in 2006, Johnny Heitinga (Netherlands) in 2010.

A16: Uruguay, Italy, England, West Germany and Argentina.

A17: Egypt.

A18: Estadio Azteca, Mexico City (1970 and 1986).

A19: Scotland (drew with Yugoslavia and Brazil, beat Zaire, went out on goal difference). Cameroon and England both achieved the same distinction in 1982. As did Belgium in 1998, and New Zealand in 2010.

A20: The referee was José Roberto Ramiz Wright, the player Mark Wright.

WORLD CUP QUIZ # 3

A1: The 1934 final, in Italy.

A2: Marcus Gayle and Robbie Earle.

A3: The Floating Leaf.

A4: David O'Leary

A5: David James (Portsmouth)

A6: It was the Croatian player Josep Šimunić in their 2006 match against Australia. Poll may have muddled him up with the similarly-named Croatian number 7 Dario Šimić, who he only booked twice, possibly after muddling him up with Australia's number 7, Brett Emerton, who he also booked twice. Šimunić was actually born and brought up in Australia, you see, which must have made it even harder to keep track.

A7: Netherlands (1998), South Korea (2002) and Australia (2006). Would have been four only Hiddink's Russia lost in a pesky play off to Slovenia in qualification for 2010.

A8: Bacary Sagna, William Gallas, Sébastien Squillaci, Abou Diaby and Gael Clichy.

A9: Morocco in 1986.

A10: Péle, Gérson, Jairzinho, Carlos Alberto, and Roberto Boninsegna.

A11: You could have... Juanito (1970), Tip & Tap (1974), Gauchito (1978), Naranjito, a walking orange (1982), Pique, a smiling jalapeno pepper (1986) Ciao, a stick man (1990), Striker, the World Cup pup (1994), Footix, a big blue cock (1998), Ato, Kaz & Nik, 'beings from the Atmozone' (2002), Goleo VI (2006) and Zakumi, a leopard with green hair (2010). Or even Fuleco, a yellow and blue armadillo, which is the 2014 pocket money magnet.

A12: Andranik Eskandarian of Iran bagged an own goal.

A13: That would be England, seven times (1954, 1962, 1970, 1982, 1986, 2002, 2006). We were also awarded eighth place in 1950, even though there weren't quarter finals that time.

A14: 1990, when West Germany beat Argentina 1-0.

A15: Uruguay.

A16: Ahn Jung-Hwan (Perugia and South Korea) had scored the goal which knocked out Italy. Gaucci is just a bad, bad loser.

A17: Tony Adams and David Rocastle.

A18: Fabio Grosso.

A19: Vuvuzelas.

A20: That 1996 Ronaldinho was actually Ronaldo, who was called Ronaldinho (little Ronaldo) originally to distinguish him from Ronaldo Rodrigues de Jesus, who was known as Ronaldão (big Ronaldo), and another teammate, Ronaldo Guiaro, who was known as Ronaldo (middle-sized Ronaldo). Then along came Ronaldinho, who was known as Ronaldinho Gaúcho (even littler Ronaldo), until both of the Ronaldinhos went to Europe to escape the confusion, and original Ronaldinho became original Ronaldo (to distinguish him from Cristiano Ronaldo), while Ronaldinho Gaúcho became Ronaldinho. See?

ABOUT THE AUTHOR

Chris England is a comedy writer, who has specialised in writing comedy about sport. His previous writing includes the stage plays (and subsequent films) *An Evening With Gary Lineker* and *Breakfast With Jonny Wilkinson*, and the books *Balham to Bollywood* and *No More Buddha, Only Football* (about the 2002 World Cup). In addition, he writes for the radio shows *7 Day Sunday* and *7 Day Saturday* for BBC Radio Five-Live, and contributed to the best-selling Pub Landlord books *The Book of British Common Sense* and *Think Yourself British* with Al Murray, The Pub Landlord.